Diana —
Thanks for your
response — Enjoy
your
Sabbath!
Charlotte

Souls at Rest

An Exploration of the Eucharistic Sabbath

In 2010, *Souls at Rest* received the
Catholic Writers Guild Seal of Approval

Charlotte Ostermann

SOULS AT REST

⊕

*An Exploration
of the Eucharistic Sabbath*

First published
by Second Spring, 2014
www.secondspring.co.uk
an imprint of Angelico Press
© Charlotte Ostermann 2014

For information, address:
Angelico Press
4709 Briar Knoll Dr.
Kettering, OH 45429
angelicopress.com

978-1-62138-091-7

Cover image: Mary Cassatt
Summertime
1894
Cover design: Michael Schrauzer

CONTENTS

A Note About the Second Edition

Since *Souls at Rest* received the Catholic Writers Guild Seal of Approval, there have been no changes in the text. This second edition is being released without the Study Guide, just to reduce the price for book groups who need multiple copies. The Complete Study Guide is available at no cost as a downloadable pdf document at soulsatleisure.com, where I have also posted my own responses to each question for anyone who is interested. I value your insights about, and responses to this work. Thanks very much for taking time to have this conversation with me and with others.

Dedication

I dedicate this book to my mother, Monteen Lucas, God rest her precious soul, who taught me to take risks; my sister, Sherri Elaine, who has always held my heart in her hands; my children Chris, Jeremy, Jared, Barbara, Hannah, Joshua, Nathan, Michael, Madeleine, and grandchildren Sophia and Dominic; to my family in the Collaborators of Your Joy, and to the Apostles of the Interior Life; to Peggy Shopen, Nancy Yacher. To all who read and gave feedback on this work in its various unpublished and first edition forms, or who interacted with me in workshops based upon these ideas, thank you very, very much. And for my husband, Russ—founder of my feast—undying gratitude for the life you provide for us, and all my love. God bless you every one!

Foreword

by Marty Barrack

"AND ON THE SEVENTH DAY God finished his work which he had done, and he rested on the seventh day from all his work which he had done. So God blessed the seventh day and hallowed it, because on it God rested from all his work which he had done in creation." The Hebrew word *shabat*, often translated rest, in fact means "cease." When God finished that work He ceased doing it. He did not tell Adam and Eve to rest; they did no work in Eden. God had blessed the seventh day, making it the Lord's Day.

God's first word to man about rest came with the manna. On the sixth day the people Israel gathered twice as much manna as usual. Moses told them why. "Tomorrow is a day of solemn rest, a holy sabbath to the Lord." This prepared the people Israel for God's third Sinai commandment, "Remember the Sabbath day, to keep it holy." The *mitzvot* of times and seasons include, "Do not travel on the Sabbath outside one's place of residence." "Sanctify the Sabbath." "Do no work on the Sabbath." "Rest on the Sabbath."

The Son of God during his mortal life lived as a devout Jew, observing the Sabbath laws. But St. Paul, also a devout Jew, wrote to the city-church in Rome, "Do you not know, brethren—for I am speaking to those who know the law—that the law is binding on a person only during his life." Death ends a Jew's obligations under the Torah. When Jesus rose from the dead, He began celebrating the Holy Sacrifice of the Mass instead, as He had in the Upper Room. But the Church Fathers tell us that He now celebrated it on the "eighth day" of the week, what we now call Sunday, the day He rose from death.

The eighth day! In ancient Hebrew gematria seven represented God's completion of His natural creation. And so Jewish apocalyptic writings describe the eighth day as a new day, a day outside creation, a supernatural day, the day of the Messiah. When the Tabernacle was complete God commanded Moses to count seven days of preparation. During those seven days Moses put up the Tabernacle each morning and took it apart each evening. On the eighth day he put it up and left it standing, and on that day the Tabernacle services began. The eighth day is also the day of the *brit milah*, circumcision, the sign of a man's entry into the Mosaic covenant.

The early Jewish Christians, seeing themselves as Jews, continued with Sabbath worship in the Temple and breaking bread in their homes. But by AD 60 they had become visibly different. Following Jesus' example, they began to celebrate the Holy Sacrifice of the Mass on the eighth day, Sunday. And in AD 70 God allowed the Temple to be destroyed.

This background illuminates for us that the Lord's Day is extraordinary, a day on which Michelangelo's great image at the center of the Sistine Chapel ceiling, in which God and man reach out to touch one another, becomes absolutely real. Each Sunday Christ gives Himself to us, whole and entire, His Body, Blood, Soul and Divinity. But the sacramental covenant of the Holy Eucharist is, as in the Sacrament of Matrimony, an exchange of persons. Christ gives Himself to us, but we also give ourselves to Him, whole and entire, our body, blood, soul and humanity. In this way we prepare for heaven, by making ourselves as much His image and likeness as we can.

Pope St. John Paul II, observing the worldwide sudden disappearance of Christianity from public life and the worldwide sudden appearance of so many hate-filled men driven to kill innocent women and children, believed that we are living today in the final confrontation between good and evil. Father John A. Hardon, SJ, his close friend and my mentor in the Faith, constantly repeated in the voice of an Old Testament prophet, "Ordinary Catholics will not survive. Only heroic Catholics will survive." Ordinary Catholics, after Sunday Mass, might perhaps watch a football game on television to relax and then go out to a restaurant for a family dinner. In the 1950s that may have been enough, but in this dark age when the demonic is all around us, we need to put on the whole armor of God at least on the Lord's Day.

Foreword

The archangel Gabriel told the Blessed Virgin, "The Holy Spirit will come upon you, and the power of the Most High will overshadow you...." (Luke 1:35). Devout Jews wear a prayer shawl with fringes called a *tallit* to enter into an intimate relationship with God. In Jewish tradition, to spread one's *tallit* over a woman is to overshadow her, to have relations with her, to become "one flesh." The Holy Spirit overshadowed the Blessed Virgin, spread His *tallit* over her, entering into an intimate marital relationship with her. Catholics have ever since called her the spouse of the Holy Spirit.

God has given us the Lord's Day as a supernatural day in which we can wrap ourselves in the Holy Spirit's *tallit* and truly give ourselves to Him as a bride gives herself to her husband, inviting His indwelling presence to enter more deeply into us. He has now sent Mrs. Charlotte Ostermann to teach us how. She calls the Lord's Day the Christian Sabbath. Strictly speaking, Sunday worship is not the Sabbath, which is the seventh day. The Holy Sacrifice of the Mass on the eighth day *fulfills* the Sabbath. But she does this to remind us that the Sabbath's ancient origins and transcendent intimacy with God remain in the Lord's Day. Jesus told us, "The sabbath was made for man, not man for the sabbath."

Catholic spiritual writers have always recognized the difference between *doing* and *being*. Holy Mother Church leads us to *be* holy. As an expression of our being holy we *do* holy things, but *being* holy is the state by which we hope to reach heaven for all eternity. Charlotte shows us that by trusting Jesus we really can wrap ourselves in the Holy Spirit's *tallit*, bringing His indwelling presence more deeply into ourselves, *becoming* tranquil in His presence. Charlotte tells us that, in the end, the Sabbath is God's poem of eternity. Come, join me on the journey to enter it.

Introduction – Finding Sunday

*The Sabbath days are a shadow of things to
come, but the body is of Christ.*
2 Colossians 16:17

THROUGH HER TEARS, a college student says to me, "I see what you mean, but I can't see how I can ever have what you describe." A family man, constantly busy serving the Church, working as a theologian, helping others grow in faith says, "Sounds great! Wish I had more time for it." A young mother laughs, "If only! Maybe when the kids are grown." What are they all talking about? What is it that is so attractive yet so "impossible"? The idea of Sabbath rest—seven and a half weeks per year of deeply refreshing rest!

The Christian Sabbath, rooted in the Jewish practice of a weekly day of rest, has the capacity to make you more human, more authentic, more alive. Created by God to give rest to the created world; amplified by His people, Israel, to prepare for the Incarnation; Sabbath has been given its Easter meaning as a place where man and God may taste the fellowship of eternity. Christ came not to abolish, but to fulfill the commandment to keep the Sabbath holy. In every way, small and large, interiorly or perceptibly, that we enter in to the Sabbath rest of Christ, we honor the Sacrifice that has made the seventh day accessible to us from within every other moment of our lives—an "eighth day" that, through us, His Body, infuses every other with peace, with Shabbat Shalom.

Life in the twenty-first century is fast-paced, noisy, complex. Because the idea of Sabbath rest seems to be the antithesis of our daily experience in this world, it may seem impossible to reconcile the realities of our busy lives with an invitation to keep one day open, still, uncluttered, holy. But this is my invitation to you nonetheless. Please come! To a day that will change your life. It was

5

created just for you by the Author of Life Himself, and corresponds perfectly to your unique personality, needs, and situation in life. That's right. Sabbath is a perfect fit for you.

Though your first thought may have been that you could not conform to a list of Sabbath demands, the truth is that Sabbath waits to conform to you. Like a bride conforming to her husband, she looks for opportunities to bless you, seeks to serve you and pour herself into such space as you will give her. So far from being a legal obligation, a list of requirements, a demand, Sabbath is like a holy servant created just for you by God, who knows you to a hair. A fuller understanding of the gift of Sabbath will enrich your prayer life, your work, your family and community relationships, your health.

I invite you to discover Shabbat Shalom—the peace of Sabbath. If you already are a Sabbath-keeper—the identifying mark of the people of God—then discover it anew.

Confronted with the beautiful ideal of Sabbath keeping, many of us shake it off as though waking from a dream. A pleasant and compelling dream, but one so rich and full of heart-breaking beauty as to seem pure fantasy. It might even feel a bit dangerous to enter too deeply into wishful thinking that contrasts so sharply with the reality of our day-to-day lives. You may feel a bit like Plato's cave-dwellers, hearing incredulously from someone who has had a glimpse outside the cave that there are real, three-dimensional beings who correspond to the shadows cast upon the cave walls—shadows they had accepted as beings in themselves. Fully conscious, intentional Sabbath keeping may seem a task for saints only—possible for religious, but hardly for lay people—threatening to the established order of lives that are too full for even one more good thing.

Yet, if you will trust one who has stepped "outside the cave" and explored the reality that is casting its weirdly dancing shadow, you will find that the genuine idea of Sabbath is earthy, practicable, realistic. Though the shadow it casts—the vague notions and feelings that arise within us—may seem alien and other-worldly, the multi-dimensional reality of Sabbath is intensely humane and ordered most particularly to our ordinary life in this world of time and space.

The worry that you haven't time to allow for richer Sabbath

observance may nag at you as you enter this study. Let me reassure you that, in calling you to keep the Sabbath holy, God is giving you time-within-time, not robbing you of time you can barely spare. You may be wary of my adding a list of superhuman requirements to a day that is already quite full, even when it is set apart and worshipful. Again, let me hasten to assure you that the Sabbath-keeping I recommend is not only possible for ordinary human beings, but takes its proportions, its scale and scope from the reality of the human person. Your needs, your limitations, your desires—combined with a growing understanding of and appreciation for Sabbath throughout this study—will be the tools and templates for your creation of a Sabbath that works for you.

Finally, you may suspect that an exploration of the idea of Sabbath rest will place you in the uncomfortable position of protecting yourself from the legalistic conclusions of an author, or study-group leader, who thinks they know how your Sabbath should look. Nothing could be further from my purposes in writing this book! My heartfelt intention is to offer you an opportunity to see more fully a gift God has given to make you more (not less!) free, more authentically yourself (not more like me!) and more abundantly alive (not more burdened by obligations!).

I have asked you to start by trusting me, because Pope St. John Paul II, in *Fides et Ratio* (Faith and Reason), describes trusting another as the first way we *know*. In Part I, I give you what I consider to be the foundational elements of a complete grasp of Sabbath: an awareness of the nature of true leisure, and a philosophy of giving practical life to the idea of holy leisure. The next way of *knowing*, of bringing fullness of form to the Idea, is by experience. In Part II, my aim is to help you find your own best ways of living the Sabbath ideal. We will look at six facets of the jewel of personhood by which you can be guided in designing your own Sabbath practices.

Having begun to more richly experience Sabbath in practical ways, you will move on to Part III, in which a further dimension—to *know* by greater intellectual engagement—adds to your growing conception of what Sabbath really is. I want you to understand more about the history and development of Sabbath, and deepen your sense of the correspondence between Sabbath and the human person. Finally, in Part IV, I help you stretch your Sabbath thinking even more as we contemplate the nature of time, the act of waiting, the formation of the soul, the meaning of education, the way of beauty, and the evangelical power of the soul at rest. I invite you to contemplate—to *know* with your whole being, letting Idea be quickened into life within you by the action of the Holy Spirit on the words you read. I highly recommend you keep a companion journal to record your insights and ideas, the development of your own thoughts and practice of Sabbath-keeping. Questions for each chapter (see: soulsatleisure.com) are for your individual journal responses, or for study-group discussion.

PART I
Foundations

1 – Wholly, Holy, Whole

My beloved speaks and says to me: "Arise, my love,
my fair one, and come away."
Song of Songs 2:10

DIAGNOSIS—to *know* through and through—is the beginning of healing. As you seek to know Sabbath thoroughly, you'll get to know the characteristics of the soul at rest, and be more aware of the weary reality of souls in the world around you. Everywhere you look, you see humanity debased, crushed, compromised and assaulted. Is it possible to make a connection between all the forms of war being waged against the very image of God in human beings? I believe so.

What mitigates against our personhood, deforms our souls, fractures and disintegrates human communities is whatever compromises true leisure. What makes us more whole, more integrated, more human? Leisure—the capacity of our souls to be at rest, to be patient, to cease acting upon and using the created world, to simply *be*. True leisure has to do with what is true about the human person—his nobility and sinfulness, the image of God he bears, his utter dependence upon grace, his deep need for genuine community, his responsiveness to beauty, and the many-layered fruitfulness of his sexuality.

You don't have to look far for examples of the restless human condition—the shape of the soul of man conditioned to an endless round of meaningless work and dissipating play. All around you, perhaps in you, the disease of the age rages: a deadly acedia—spiritual impotence, moral lassitude, indifference to truth and beauty, debilitating despair. Early Church Fathers called acedia the "noonday demon" as it feels so like the midday slump we often experience in our energy for getting our work done. Meaning literally, "without care," acedia, or sloth, is "not mere idleness or laziness; it involves a *torpor animi*, a dullness of the soul that can stem from restlessness just as easily as from indolence."[1] Dante's *Inferno* depicts "those afflicted by acedia . . . as suffering from *lento amore*, a slow love that cannot motivate and uplift, leaving the soul stagnant, unable to move under the heavy burden of sin."[2]

Sabbath is the cure for the ills caused by neglect of God, by distracting busyness, by impatient haste, by the assault of noise and by running away from who we truly are. The key to better understanding of what kinds of activities to engage in or to avoid on Sunday, is this: the human person. God created this day of rest for you, for human beings, so to find out what makes it *holy*, we must look at what makes people *whole*.

To restore the human soul and the culture that flows from it for good or ill, we must first examine the sin of sloth. Profound rest is needed, but to appropriate it, we must know what is fighting against that rest.

Sloth, or acedia, is the unheralded, almost hidden, besetting sin of our times—unheralded because it is misunderstood; hidden because its symptoms are disguised or misdiagnosed; and besetting us all to some degree because we have overlooked a mighty, God-given cure. It is, as the Church fathers taught, deadly. It strikes at the very roots of our freedom—at human dignity itself. Sabbath rest cannot be understood or appreciated apart from awareness of this sin that undermines everything Sabbath was created to give to the human person for his edification and development.

Before we explore what St. Thomas Aquinas taught about sloth, let me digress briefly to caution you against diagnosing the sin of sloth wherever you notice the condition of listlessness, depression, moral indifference, or even laziness (though the word sloth has become synonymous in our day with the word laziness). Just as drunkenness is both a sin and a condition—the latter an observable phenomenon and the former a matter privileged with the privacy of the confessional—so we may observe and address the fact of debilitating lassitude, or of other symptoms of acedia, without presuming

---

1. R. R. Reno, "Fighting the Noonday Devil," *First Things*, Aug/Sept 2003, 31–36.
2. Ibid.

the need for confession of sin in any other person. We'll likely need our priest's help unraveling our own culpability, much less another person's. Finding the symptoms in ourselves should never lead to self-condemnation, but to a more searching examination of conscience. In all your dealings with persons afflicted by acedia—yourself *or* others—your charity in leading a soul to Sabbath rest is of the utmost importance.

Now, to the bracing tonic of St. Thomas' wisdom. I described sloth as misunderstood and, indeed, your first reaction to hearing it is the "disease" for which Sabbath is the "cure" may have been, "That can't be me! I never slack off and I'm always busy doing worthwhile things." You are correct in linking laziness to sloth, but St. Thomas agreed with earlier saints such as Gregory and Isidore that a deeper spiritual sorrow was the deadly root from which sloth's "daughters" (such as laziness) grew. Sloth is "an oppressive sorrow which . . . so weighs upon man's mind that he wants to do nothing. . . . Hence sloth implies a certain weariness of work. . . ."[3]

Even the holy person experiences the "noonday devil"—a midday slump of sluggish, work-weariness—feelings which, like feelings of sadness, are not in themselves sinful. The particular sorrow to which Thomas refers is an avoidance of spiritual goods, a failure to take pleasure in those things which please God and, thus, to do whatever love of God calls us to do. We can flee the Divine Good—fail to do acts of virtue for God's sake—by pursuing other pleasures, by shirking hard or distasteful work, by dilly-dallying in keeping the commandments, by "rushing after various things without rhyme or reason,"[4] by daydreaming, by constant physical or mental movement, and by incessant talking. Now it becomes easier to see why sloth is hidden from our gaze. If we look only for evidence of "laziness" in ourselves, we may believe acedia is not affecting us. But if we wonder (and allow God to help us discern) about our busyness, the constant stream of activities and distractions, our lukewarmness

---

3. St. Thomas Aquinas, *Summa Theologica*, II-2-Q35, Article 1: Answer to Objection 4.
4. Ibid, Article 4: Reply to Objection 3.

or downright indifference to spiritual goods, we may be surprised to find we need help fighting sloth after all.

This deadly spiritual lassitude is both the cause of and the result of our attitude toward leisure. Josef Pieper, in *Leisure, the Basis of Culture*, develops the concept of true leisure as an antidote to the dissipation and spiritual stagnation of sloth. Pieper paints a picture of man debased and dehumanized by lack of understanding of what it means to be fully, richly human. The person divorced by education or societal conditions from the sense that he has been created not to perform a function, but to bear the very image of God, is likely to experience the spiritual and emotional malaise of acedia. Lacking a sense of his own transcendent *being*, he is prone either to an over-*doing* which leaves him inwardly barren, or to an exclusive focus upon the pleasures of earthly life, which accomplishes the same inward emptiness.

For the human person to flourish, a very different sense of leisure is needed—one which flows directly from the provision of Sabbath refreshment by God for man's highest good. Not sufficient for the human soul are activities that merely distract and entertain, or celebrations that fail to lift the consciousness toward its Creator and its eternal destiny. We will be, Pieper argues, most vibrantly, profoundly alive when we are able to be at leisure with ourselves—to be alone with God and at rest in Him. Our worship, then, and the Sabbath rest flowing from it, is what makes us whole, holy, wholly ourselves.

All around us our inward being is made manifest in the form of the culture we create. This culture—our arts, institutions, traditions, celebrations and laws—reflects, on a community scale, our personal interior harmony, or lack thereof. These cultural elements in turn provide the context for the formation of our souls. It matters very much whether our hearts, minds, souls and bodies are well integrated by virtue of true worship, of holistic love of God. The virtue that opposes sloth is fervent love. What we are, we create more of. The more Shabbat Shalom, Sabbath peace, fills us, the more it fills our world.

St. Thomas considered sloth a sin against the commandment to keep the Sabbath holy. Whether inflamed by indolence or by restless busyness, sloth is spiritual laziness and renders us impotent to wield ourselves in spiritual struggle. It at first seems surprising to propose rest as an antithesis to laziness, but Aquinas positions a true rest against a false; a God-given rest against one taken and abused; a refreshing pause against a debilitating laziness; an immersion in the recreating and joyful rest of God against the consuming distraction of ceaseless activity. "Leisure is not justified in making the functionary as 'trouble-free' in operation as possible, . . . but rather in keeping the functionary *human*."[5] Our very understanding of what it means to be a human person is rooted in our right understanding of ourselves not as workers—components of the productive machineries of man—but as image-bearers of the glory of revelation that infuses our soul in leisure understood as worship. The flame of zeal that quickens the "functionary" into the human person thrives in the atmosphere of the Sabbath.

Sabbath rest is essential to worship of God and to fellowship with Him. It is crucial to the formation of your soul, to the right ordering of all your activity, and to your preparation for eternity. It is a gift given by Jesus—Lord Sabbaoth—to aerate the "soil" of your life, allowing grace to permeate and the Word to flourish there. Sabbath is a hologram of eternity within time, and only the soul shaped by its presence, its spaciousness, can fully apprehend reality. Sabbath is the medicine for many of the ills of the post-modern world, and we keepers are the channels through which its waters bless the desert around us. Sabbath calls the soul to its Lover, the world to its Creator, and the human being to his full personhood by its supernatural beauty.

5. Josef Pieper, *Leisure, the Basis of Culture* (San Francisco, CA: Ignatius Press, 2001).

2 – Taking the Cure

*While it is true that we cannot base our security on any form
that embodies the mystery, it is also true that any value
which has not taken on a specific form, or is not tending
toward one will inevitably tend to disappear over time.*
Fr. Luigi Giussani, "The Risk of Education"

BEFORE YOU BEGIN, in Part II, to consider the practical steps
you might take to enrich your Sabbath-keeping, let's consider a few obstacles and questions you may face as you move
forward. Remember, we are laying the foundation here for the
secure and beautiful "home" we hope to build of the Sabbath idea.
Just as medicines taken incautiously can act as poisons, so the Sabbath cure for acedia has its own risks.

The danger of designing your, or your family's, practice of Sabbath is that you will do it badly. You'll bring into Shabbat the stress,
the restlessness, the mental clutter, the zeal for action and pro-
grams, the fears, the smallness of your soul. Yet even so, you will not
mar its beauty, but you will be transformed by it—"transformed by
the renewing of your mind" (Rom 12:2). G.K. Chesterton tells us
that, "a thing worth doing is worth doing badly"—in one pithy
stroke slaying our performance orientation, our pride. It takes some
humility to begin at all, to take a small symbolic step, to stumble,
bumble clumsily and fall. But Sabbath is a "thing" abundantly
worth "doing," even badly.

The greater danger is to nod in agreement with the grand Idea of
Sabbath rest, then to remain unchanged. "For if any one is a hearer
of the word and not a doer, he is like a man who observes his natural face in a mirror; for he observes himself and goes away and at
once forgets what he was like. But he who looks into the perfect law,
the law of liberty, and perseveres, being no hearer that forgets, but a
doer that acts, he shall be blessed in his doing" (James 1:23–25).

Ideas left to themselves within the intellect fail to engage us as persons, as whole, embodied beings. They can be stimulating (far more so, perhaps, than whatever calls for our attention in the world around us), but if we are not stimulated to respond, to risk the frustration of somehow bringing the Idea (the Virtue, the Work of Art, the Reality) into being, then they die, or can become idols. Imagination becomes "vain" when it fails to take form, to have effect in our real world.

Practice—small, specific, concrete actions you take to invest the week, the day, the vocation, the work you do with Sabbath meaning—makes perfect; perfects the shape of the Idea within your person so that you may be molded by it. Ironically, there simply isn't enough time to pursue all the worthwhile practices that can be suggested as ways to make the Sabbath more genuinely refreshing. The need for deep rest is widely acknowledged, and ideas for relaxation are plentiful. But only if you seek out Sabbath's implications for the whole person—body and soul entwined—will you enter in to the truly holistic, wholeness-producing, rest of Shabbat Shalom.

Many voices are calling to us to enter some form of deep restfulness. From doctors, alternative medical practitioners, teachers of attention-challenged students, Buddhists, Muslims, Jews, sleep deprivation investigators, corporate power nappers, massage therapists and psychologists, the cry resounds. "Tiredness is one of our strongest, most noble and instructive feelings, yet it has become a matter of shame! Everywhere we see people overcoming their exhaustion and pushing on with intensity—cultivating the great mass mania which all around is making life so hard and so utterly graceless."[1] "[R]est should be restored as a prized color in our paint box of remedies and cures."[2]

Though I, too, invite you into the deep physical and mental rest of Sabbath, I caution you to beware of focusing only upon its many proven health benefits. When we move toward any goal-oriented Sabbath practice, we flatten Sabbath somewhat. As Martin Buber would say, it moves from being a "You" to an "It," and we move

1. Michael Leunig, "Learn to Rest," *Resurgence*, #202.
2. Ann Japenga, "The Siesta Cure," *Alternative Medicine*, Jan/Feb 2004, 77–79.

from encounter with a whole, complex, living Reality, to manipulation of a thing for our own ends. Since we bring to practice our disequilibrium, this subtle balance will have to be restored again and again. Our lust for progress will be frustrated over and over again as Sabbath slowly, slowly takes shape within us and within our lives. By ordering our Sabbath practice toward God, we keep its greatest gift central and from this center our practice is best developed. "It is faith alone which gives access to its deeper meaning and ensures that it will not become banal and trivialized."[3]

You may find yourself resisting the very idea of consciously creating your Sabbath. After all, isn't it a day just to go with the flow? Unfortunately, the intrusion of reason into the "free and spontaneous" dimension of human emotions or recreations has come in our day to seem as unattractive as a dictatorial tour bus guide propelling us relentlessly through a "vacation." Though we want to avoid the forced march, it would be a shame to miss some of the richest treasures of this new place for lack of any planning at all, when we have such a short stay in mind. Just as you are most free when reason can command your natural passions, on Sabbath you will be most free to act as you please when you've spent time genuinely considering what pleases you, and why.

It is more important than you might think to differentiate the concept of Sabbath rest from the modern notion of the "weekend." "Unfortunately, when Sunday loses its fundamental meaning and becomes merely part of a 'weekend', it can happen that people stay locked within a horizon so limited that they can no longer see 'the heavens.' Hence, though ready to celebrate, they are really incapable of doing so."[4] Acedia born of muddling the meaning of Sunday robs us of the capacity to celebrate Christ's resurrection, to participate in Mass with full engagement. For Christians, the Eucharist is the wellspring of all joy and central to all our practices.

Communal delight and celebration—Easter joy—overshadows even restedness as the defining characteristic of a Sabbath well kept.

---

3. Pope St. John Paul II, *Dies Domini*, Paragraph 13.
4. Ibid., Paragraph 4.

Just by setting apart time for Sunday worship together, we are detaching ourselves from the chores, ball games, concerts and self-seeking that clamor for our attention. For a while, at least, we cease doing to focus on what Christ has done; cease moving to be still and present with Him; create silence filled only by His voice; escape the loneliness of separate lives to live as one Body. In the Eucharist is, literally, the fullness of the idea of Sabbath—tasted, experienced, intimately received. Whatever else we do or refrain from doing to participate in sanctifying the day must be informed by, must flow from the moment of communion in which we are most fully whole, most human.

We will have to make plans—conscious choices—to be ready for a Sabbath of rest. Paradoxically, we must add to our Monday-through-Saturday activities whatever preparation and planning is necessary to "make straight the way of the Lord" on Sunday. This seemingly impossible paradox is resolved first by default, then by intention, and gradually by the practices we adopt. At first, when you determine to attend Mass and to stop whatever is your typical, daily work (wage-earning, schoolwork, housekeeping), the impossibility of carving out one day is simply settled by default. A useful analogy to this process comes from marriage.

If divorce is an option for a couple, then the decision *not* to divorce will have to be made over and over, during good times and bad. The likelihood is that the strength of one or the other spouse to resist the option of divorce may be overcome by its apparent attractiveness during a low point. If Sunday is perceived as another day we may use to get work accomplished—if the option is always open to fill it with the inevitable overflow of activity from our workaday lives—then we will be faced weekly with the daunting task of choosing to "do nothing" in the face of so many things that all shout with a voice of urgency to be done. We are most likely to cave in under the pressure of unfinished "to do" lists, deadlines and "hot fires." Do you see that first, you must decide to set apart the day and be willing to resolve the issues that clamor for your attention in some other way besides profaning its holiness?

Of course, if you must work on Sunday to save lives, or serve the Church, your rest may need to come on another day. And if you simply cannot separate an entire day at this point, you must begin with smaller, even symbolic, Sabbath observance. The Eucharist alone has such power to rest our souls and effectively change them, that it should be the starting point, no matter what else you manage to do to celebrate the Sabbath. Growing in your awareness of the gift of Sabbath, you will grow in understanding of the gift of the Eucharist, and the practice of honoring the obligation to attend Mass will be tremendously fruitful. The wonderful thing about even the smallest stand you make for the truth of your personhood, the truth of your need for time to receive your being from Christ, is that it subtly affects every other aspect of your life for good. You are free to make whatever response is authentic for you to the invitation to the Lord's Day and to His Table. You will grow in freedom in the measure of this response.

To say that you are "free to do whatever you want" before you have begun cultivating true freedom (that which can only come of this most human capacity for leisure and for Truth) is to remain forever in some degree of bondage. Only the person able to be at leisure is truly free. Once you have created at least the space for the Eucharist and, preferably, the space also for true and resurrecting delight in being *not* a worker, a cog in a machine, a human resource, a functionary, or a consumer, but a human person, you will begin to reap the benefits of Sabbath rest. The fires that seemed to threaten destruction, the deadlines that loomed, the duties that had to be performed will all be resolved in one way or another without recourse to use of the Sabbath.

Perhaps you will have disappointed someone, lost a valuable contract, received a lower grade, admitted that you cannot be all things to all people, missed a meeting, or in some other way felt a loss caused by your Sabbath-keeping. But, somehow, life will have gone on, and you will have put yourself on the road to a life not dictated to you by deadlines and duties—a life in the Spirit, of freedom and creativity. Let these losses teach you detachment from the expectations and regard of others, from your pride in your own capabilities and perfections, from whatever material gain you have forfeited. Welcome to humanity—where not everything can legitimately be accomplished, where we can't always have our way, or do all things well; where some things (many things!) are more valuable than possessions or prestige, and where time is decidedly *not* money!

Every "Sabbath" practice could be a daily one, but the danger is that, by making them "anytime," we will make for them no time. If you feel apathetic, indifferent toward the saints, other people, or toward virtue, that is a sign of the deadly acedia for which Shabbat Shalom is the cure. "Busyness is a principal source, reinforcement and excuse for our indifference; our times are inventive in devising narcotics, but we have yet to find any drug more powerful than busyness.... When my brother or sister has become a stranger to me ... then I have become a stranger to myself."[5] Recognize your indifference as a symptom of disease and stop whatever else you are doing to find the cure.

A dangerous temptation of starting to keep the Sabbath more *wholly* is to compare yourself with others. It is natural to feel some frustration that our friends aren't making the same choices, practicing the same austerities, interpreting Sabbath in the same way. We long for community that respects and fosters our Sabbath-keeping, but if we are to grow into the fullness of our own freedom, we must respect theirs. If our focus is on what we are giving up, we are likely to resent those who make different Sabbath choices. If we keep Sabbath in a spirit of circling our wagons against a hostile culture, our rest will never bless that culture. But if we focus on the delights in store for us as we come closer and closer to the still center, the interior chapel where He meets us, then we will grow detached from what others do or do not do—freedom, indeed!

If your life seems to be a tangled mess, you may be tempted to wait until you've got your "act together" before moving on to what seems an "advanced" spiritual practice. I caution you strongly that a life without genuine Sabbath rest is a life becoming more, not less, tangled! Sabbath is the key to, not the prize for, getting life's priorities and activities in order. Think of easing the tension on a rope or

---

5. David Bailey Harned, *Patience: How We Wait Upon the World* (Boston, MA: Cowley Publications, 1997).

necklace to get the knots out.[6] The competitive, impatient, performance anxiety we bring to work, homemaking, or college classes will color our experience of Sabbath.

The person new to slowing down life's pace may feel restless and bored with an un-busy day. Accustomed to quick switching among a variety of activities, and the gratification of goals rapidly achieved, he has developed what amounts to attention deficit disorder. Unable to stay in one place long—mentally, or physically—without discomfort, his deficiency is exposed by the revelation of Sabbath. Faced with the provision of long, slow hours of unstructured time, Masses and meals that threaten to "go on forever," and handcrafts that take days or weeks to do what a machine could do in minutes, he grows antsy for results, progress, change, speed. This impatience extends to his desire for change in himself. "We live in an age of impatience, an age which in everything, from learning the ABC to industry, tries to cut out and do away with the natural season of growth. This is why so much in our life is abortive. We ought to let everything grow in us, as Christ grew in Mary. And we ought to realize that in everything that does grow quietly in us, Christ grows."[7]

It will be helpful, as an antidote to the interior demand for rapid progress, to realize and cultivate the value of the small, small change characteristic of true growth. Jacques Barzun points out that, though the term "quantum leap" is commonly used to describe a revolutionary, huge change, its actual meaning in physics refers to the smallest possible change.[8] The movement of one electron to a neighboring orbital, the quantum leap is the indivisible, infinitesimal change that reorders and revolutionizes the material world, one atom at a time.

A Japanese word, "kaizen," meaning "incremental change toward the end you desire," suggests that "kaizen" is at once the smallest

6. Note: There is a devotion to "Mary, Who Unties Knots" which has been a particular blessing to me.

7. Caryll Houselander, *The Reed of God* (Allen, TX: Christian Classics, Division of Resources for Christian Living, no date shown), 37.

8. Jacques Barzun, *From Dawn to Decadence: 500 Years of Western Cultural Life, 1500 to the Present* (New York, NY: HarperCollins, 2000).

and the best step you can take, because it is the change which is truly do-able and sustainable for you. You can dream all day about having become a slower, more centered, deliberate person, but until you actually incorporate your intention—make it real through action—the dream has no power to effect lasting change. Scripture teaches us not to "despise the day of small beginnings" (Zech 4:10), recognizing that a small step is more helpful than a grand idea.

Bill Murray's character in the movie *Groundhog Day*, once reconciled to endlessly repeating the same ordinary day, realizes that he can accumulate abundant changes in his skills, attitudes, and relationships by incorporating new values little by little into the activities of one small day. The majestic tree grows in a spiral—in endless circles seemingly going nowhere—upward in gradual, almost imperceptible steps toward the sky. The beautiful opal is formed as, drop by slow drop, mineral-filled water accumulates underground. As you begin to value Sabbath rest, worship, slowness, community, food, and to incorporate—literally, to embody—this value in small, even symbolic, acts, you start to reverse the downward spiral of acedia.

You will, doubtless, be frustrated sometimes by your slow progress, by the discrepancy between what you are and what you imagine you could be, and by the interference of other people in your best attempts to change and grow. Remember, though, that frustration is the chronic condition of impatient souls, and give yourself some slack—permission to grow by fits and starts, and to regress in one practice while growing in another. You'll find your humility and your patience with others both increase. This is the gift of Sabbath—the interior space where you and others are safe to become whole.

As you take up the study of practical ways of expressing your Sabbath intentions, expect an adventure! What you begin to do in trust, believing there is something to this idea, will nourish the idea within you and develop the momentum of your own desire. Once you get over the shock of taking the day "out of play" and realize that the consequences are not only bearable but decidedly positive, your intention to do this on a weekly basis establishes a rhythm of remembrance and expectation. Fresh from a restful Sunday, as you re-enter the maelstrom of the week, you carry with you a new perspective on all your activities. The memory of one day restfully lived tempers your restlessness.

Your work is done a bit more consciously and your addiction to distraction is somewhat abated. You are less alone in the world, having dwelt for a time in community—with friends and family, and with Our Eucharistic Lord. Even if you are caught up in the whirl of demands and events, as you move away from the still center of the week, the Sabbath pulls you back from the edge. It begins to call to you mid-week, promising rest and refreshment. Its reminder of your human dignity lifts your soul despite the weight of menial, boring, or unappreciated work. Just as the Jews looked back toward the Sabbath from Monday till Wednesday, and toward its next interlude from Wednesday till Friday, you will begin to look forward to each blessed Sunday. Soon the fragrance of Shabbat Shalom will infuse the entire week.

PART II
Experience the Sabbath

*By wisdom a house is built, and by understanding
it is established; by knowledge the rooms are filled
with all precious and pleasant riches.*
Proverbs 24:3

*You now have laid a foundation of forethought upon which to build
the structure of your Sabbath practice. Having first known by trusting me, to some extent, you want to move on—to know by experiencing the gifts of the day of rest, through conscientious choice of what
you will do, or not do. From the Jewish understanding of Shabbat, we
learn that both doing and non-doing make the Sabbath holy; set it
apart from every other day. Two words are used in Scriptural Sabbath commandments (Ex. 20:18, Deut. 5:12)—"to observe" (or
"keep") and "to remember" the Sabbath. From these and other
Scriptural interpretations, Jewish Sabbath practices and prohibitions
were derived.*

*No longer bound to legalistic observance, we must each create our
own response to the holiness of our Sabbath day. Like a jewel in a
beautiful setting, Eucharistic communion with our Lord is enhanced
by our attitude and approach to the rest of the day. However we
decide to remember the Sabbath and keep it holy will be less important than our intent to, by these practices, "grow up in all things unto
Christ" (Eph 4:15) and to become whole so that we may love Him
wholly.*

*Discovering and recovering our capacity for true leisure is the
prescription for becoming more fully who we truly are—more fully
alive as individuals, families, communities of believers. Rather than
give you a laundry list of "things to do on Sunday," then, I want to
make suggestions based on six principles of personhood—ways in
which Sabbath corresponds beautifully to what it means to be a person, to be you. In each of the following chapters I will hold up for*

your consideration one of these aspects of being, give examples of seemingly opposite ways of being out of balance in each area, and share ideas for Sabbath practices tailored to your specific needs for restoring interior equanimity.

It won't be possible to "take the cure" without considering who you are, what you need, and what you desire. This can be a little daunting if you have struggled against giving in to selfish desires, or to change a troubling part of your personality, or to ignore your own needs in order to serve others. I assure you, you do not need to worry that surrendering your whole, true, imperfect self to Sabbath rest will undermine the efforts you are making be more responsible, or less self-centered, or more generous. Shabbat Shalom—the peace of Sabbath rest—is offered by the Great Physician, to meet you right where you are, right now. Loosen the reins now, and let Him help you steer your course.

3 – Be a Place

Our present state of being denotes "exile", temporary displacement;
its end, however, marks "redemption", homecoming.
Pinchas Peli, "Shabbat Shalom"

THE DIGNITY of the human person consists in his very *being*. The very fact of his existence conveys into the world a flash of the glory of the "I Am," whose image he bears. Yet how many of us are at complete ease just *being*, without activity to distract us from, or to justify, our existence? Our interior demand for activity makes us impatient with ourselves and others. Our inability to respond to ourselves or to others as a tabernacle of God's Presence makes us unable to respond to the demands of spiritual growth. "[O]n the Sabbath we especially care for the seed of eternity planted in the soul."[1] Its growth results in an expansiveness, a dimensionality, of the soul that can be thought of as *place*.

Each of us has the capacity to be *place* for others. The interior spaciousness and integrity of that place is a measure of the formation of our soul. Henri Nouwen taught that one of the crucial tasks of spiritual growth is the "movement from hostility to hospitality."[2] In creating the Sabbath for man, God has "made place" within Himself for us to dwell in perfect peace. We are thus taught and brought to exercise that same heart hospitality for others.

Martin Buber, in the classic and beautiful book *I and Thou*, speaks of the vast difference between perceiving a person as an "It" (which we ignore, manipulate, use, abuse) and encountering another as a "You" (a multi-dimensional, awesome reality). "When I

1. Abraham Joshua Heschel, *The Sabbath: Its Meaning for Modern Man* (New York, NY: Farrar, Strauss and Giroux, 1951).
2. Henri Nouwen, *Reaching Out* (Garden City, NY: Doubleday & Company, 1975).

confront a human being as my You ... then he is no thing among things, nor does he consist of things. ... Neighborless and seamless, he is You and fills the firmament. Not as if there were nothing but he, but everything else lives in *his* light. Even as a melody is not composed of tones, nor a verse of words, nor a statue of lines—one must pull and tear to turn a unity into a multiplicity—so it is with the human being to whom I say You."[3] The impatient, or indifferent soul—burdened by acedia—has little capacity to encounter the fullness of another person, another You, much less to encounter the Person of Christ.

The more we deprive our souls of Sabbath rest, the more narrow, cramped, inhospitable, and flat they become. True community can only thrive when we make time for one another, and give each other place within our hearts. Time and place are thus linked together in the virtue of patience, without which community collapses. Both our indifference to others and our impatience with them close the door of our hearts, rendering us and them homeless, in a sense. "[T]he two vices that are juxtaposed against patience ... turn both the self and other people into displaced persons. ... In their shared indifference to patience and the room it always offers other people, [indifference and impatience] are pervasive sources of the dislocation and dispossession that foster generations of displaced persons."[4]

Sabbath holds the key that can free us and those whose lives we touch from the lonely prison—a corrective to busyness, sloth, apathy and hostility. "Busyness is a principal source, reinforcement and excuse for our indifference. ... The vices that are ranged against patience lead to dispossession, the loss of the self ... vice isolates the self and thereby deprives it of any hope of richness in itself, so does it cause the self to project its own poverty upon the world."[5]

3. Martin Buber, *I and Thou*, Walter Kaufman, trans., S.G. Smith, trans. (New York, NY: Simon & Schuster Adult Publishing Group, 1971).

4. David Bailey Harned, *Patience: How We Wait Upon the World* (Boston, MA: Cowley Publications, 1997).

5. Ibid.

David Bailey Harned, in *Patience*, gives us—we who understand leisure "not as a quantity of time" but as a "condition of the soul"— the key to the cultivation of the joyful rest of God, the sabbatine center and fountain of our humanity. He says, "[p]atience must always lie at the center of leisure, for reality does not disclose its secrets to careless, hasty, or indifferent scrutiny."[6] "The ceaseless activity that is so often the other side of our incapacity to enjoy leisure has its source, strange as it initially may seem, in impatience and laziness, in the sloth which ... expresses itself either in withdrawal from others or else in relentless busyness that enables the self to hide from itself."[7] Not fully present to self, or to other people, we ultimately fail to be present to Christ.

Sabbath asks us to relinquish some of our incessant doing, and—in contrast to laziness in the pursuit of spiritual goods—to be keenly, joyously present to God's Presence. We tend to err in the direction of one extreme, or the other, moving in either case away from the *via media*, the point of balance. I suggest you choose Sabbath practices that act as tonics to your natural inclination either to over-activity, or to indolence. If your focus during the week is typically external to your own center, your own home, take up forms of non-doing to sanctify the Sabbath.

Declare a no homework day; spend time at home making few demands upon your self and others; avoid imposing your will, getting things accomplished, bending creation to your designs. Extend your time in contemplative prayer; gaze upon icons with receptivity to the Holy Spirit who brings them to life; enjoy *lectio divina*—long, quiet meditation upon morsels of Scripture. Spend an hour in adoration before the Blessed Sacrament.

Adrienne Von Speyr recommends the practice of Marian prayers such as the rosary to help us create quiet interior chambers of encounter with the person of Christ: "[C]hristians can find only in the hidden silence of Mary's heart the true access to the interior world of the son. Precisely the Marian prayers ... need and create

6. Ibid.
7. Ibid.

peace, distance, time."[8] Father Benedict Groeschel also calls the rosary "a place." We can think of these prayers as time spent within a chapel that, by its structure, contributes to the shaping of our souls in receptive spaciousness. "The innermost point of our world,... that axis upon which our self, our soul and its outlying persons all turn, is Shabbat," says Hebrew scholar Yanki Tauber.[9]

If you are typically more inwardly focused during the week—acting primarily "on your own account"—hiding, to some degree, from self-giving encounter with other people, take a Sabbath rest from yourself and your own concerns. Pray for the capacity to be present and responsive to someone each Sunday: take a meal to a new mom; read to a child; visit the sick; pray for a particular mission or country; serve at a soup kitchen. Work on handmade gifts that take a "month of Sundays" to complete. Pray a full rosary for the intentions of friends; hand-deliver a bouquet of flowers; write an actual, physical, old-fashioned letter.

Only you will know if your restraint from activity is resulting in your becoming more fully present to and surrendered to Christ, or whether self-giving is making you more acutely aware of His Presence in other people. In the Eucharist you are given a glimpse of the capacity of a human Person to be at once completely self-possessed and completely donated to another. Carry that example with you to marvel at and to follow during the rest of your Sabbath day.

8. Adrienne von Speyr, *Handmaid of the Lord*, E.A. Nelson, trans. (San Francisco, CA: Ignatius Press, 1985).
9. Yanki Tauber, "The Axis," at www.chabad.org/253215.

4 – Be Quiet

The disciple should be silent and listen.
St. Benedict

To simply *be*, is to be a place of encounter with God. The chief quality of this place is its serenity, its freedom from clamor. Between the two extremes of negation—empty silence—and deafening noise, lies the quality of quietude—a listening calm at the core of our humanity. This quiet chapel at the center of our soul enables us to hear God's still, small voice, and to hear our own. The world we live in is so constantly full of noise that our inner ears (and sometimes our physical ears as well) grow dull and deaf in self-defense. It becomes difficult for us to be calm when quiet feels like an empty vacuum and seems threatening or impersonal. Just as the sounds of his mother doing dishes comfort the child trying to fall asleep in his dark, quiet room, so the sounds of traffic, radio, television, idle chatter reassure us that we are not alone in the vast and terrifying world. The greater the displacement, the insecurity, the alienation of our souls, the more difficult it will be to separate ourselves from the din.

If yours tends to be a noisy life, let Sabbath be the day you turn off the media, keep a Grand Silence for part of the day, or refuse to answer the phone. Look for ways in which you are making it difficult for others to have a say and, on Sunday, make intentional—even if symbolic—gestures of suppressing the noises that help you avoid their messages. Perhaps this is the day for a family meeting, a state-of-the-union talk with your spouse and each child, or calling to visit with an aging parent. Spend time outdoors being hushed by the wonders of creation. Deliberately, consciously lower your voice on Sundays; write your instructions to the kids instead of yelling them; use a little bell to call the family to eat or to leave for Mass; make a game of seeing who can be quietest or go the longest without speaking.

Some forms of meditation encourage the suppression of all interior "voices" clamoring to be heard within your soul. To the extent that confusion, vain imaginings, and interior strife are quieted, this may be helpful. To the extent that this practice attempts to negate reality, or makes thoughtlessness a good higher than truth, it has the effect of deafening us as certainly as noise does to meaningful messages. True, humane quietude must be cultivated as a capacity for hearing, and for discerning meaning in what is heard, not as an ability to ignore.

Our own being sometimes cries out in physical ailments to be heard, to be attended to. In the tumult of our lives the most important messages are most often the ones we are tuning out. We suppress or ignore them at our peril. For this reason, I suggest you take time on the Sabbath to listen and attend to the wisdom of your body. Journal about the aches and pains and dreams you've been having. Ask God to help you hear and respond to the needs they reveal. Awaken your senses—light Sabbath candles; burn incense as you pray; play music that helps your soul to soar in praise to God; set a beautiful table; smell the bouquet and the baking bread; wear clothing that makes Sunday feel special; bathe in a tub sprinkled with essential oils; massage your feet.

Take time on Sundays to appreciate the created world—touch it, draw it, inhale it, taste it, listen to it. It may seem odd to connect Sabbath sensuality with your need for interior quietude, but we do not benefit by a silence bought at the cost of suppressing reality. Each sense is a point of contact with the real world; even pain is a message about what *is*. Both suppression of and distraction from such messages can signal our deep fear of our own or others' neediness; of truth we need to hear from our own divided being, or from God. Quietude implies profound trust in God. If you sense fearful disquiet in your soul, make Sunday the day you entrust all the needs of the world to God in trust through the Divine Mercy chaplet— "Jesus, I trust in You." Save the Sunday paper until Monday if the news tends to upset you, or take a list of the distressing items to Mass, offering them up in prayer as your Mass intention or with a post-Mass rosary decade.

The French Marianist Father Ven. William Joseph Chaminade

designed five disciplines of silence not for monks, but for active lay people: The Silence of Words—saying only what is edifying to others and fit to utter in the Presence of the Lord; the Silence of Signs—communicating respect for others through attention to the non-verbal messages we send; the Silence of the Mind—discretion in the consumption of media messages and careless conversation; the Silence of the Passions—avoidance of overindulgence in emotions; the Silence of the Imagination—monitoring the scenarios and day-dreams that play on our "mental screen." All such disciplines flower within the discipline of Sabbath-keeping.

As the body is slowed and stilled, and clamor is quieted, practice perfects our ability to recollect our equanimity and poise in the Presence of our ever-patient, ever-waiting Lord. Such a Sabbath moment, hour, or day is a deep pool of refreshment and renewal. As your commitment to Sabbath-keeping grows, you will be blessed with greater and greater sensitivity to the need of your soul for silence. As you learn to long for interior stillness into which you may more easily welcome God, you might pray, with the Psalmist, for Him to still and quiet your soul within you, like a child at his mother's breast (Ps. 131:2 paraphrase).

Finally, give thought each Sunday to the words of blessing you may be forgetting to say. Write thank-you notes; give hugs; ask God for a new way to give a message that hasn't been received; think what compliments you have forgotten to voice. In the Blessed Sacrament we have the example of Our Lord both utterly, quietly receptive to hearing all our concerns and also uttering the word of healing to our listening souls.

5 – Be Slow

*Patience is the work of single-mindedness: the eye of the mind
is concentrated on one thing alone, in contrast to the distracted busyness that is incapable of pausing in order to see the world as
it is and not only as we would have it be.*
David Bailey Harned, "Patience"

OUR CULTURE both expresses and perpetuates the health or
disease, integrity or disintegration of our souls. An honest
look at it serves as a diagnostic tool—a measure of our society's collective spiritual health. To the extent my own life embodies
the themes I see manifest all around me in the prevailing culture, I
am contributing to it. What little I can do to effect change must
begin in the stillness and silence of my own soul. A constant feature
of the culture of our times is speed. Speed is a particular form of
disquietude, of impatience, of displacement.

Our cars and planes, news, gigabytes, optical signals, radio waves,
and money all fly from one place to another in a frenzy of competition for our attention. In our hurry we speed past landscapes and
people without seeing them. Medicines quell symptoms quickly
and thousands of products gratify us immediately. In the process of
getting so much seemingly accomplished so fast, we race past our
very selves. With no time to dwell, to ponder, to wait, to prepare
food with loving attention, our souls lose dimension, lose some of
the quality of being vessels for grace. Remember, it takes time for
person to become *place*. As we war in haste against patience, we war
against personhood as well.

The Old English root of the word "haste" actually means "violence" and so is an appropriate word for the rash, headlong rush to
move past "now" and "here," past ourselves and our loved ones.
"Haste is the pathos of active, arbitrary people and, as such, is in
contrast with wonder, which halts and looks. . . . Haste is a form of

rage."[1] Our orientation toward production and away from process contributes to our haste to become "finished products" and to reach a point in an imaginary future that is always just enough to distract us from every moment that is now, that is real, that can be filled with grace. "Speed . . . is a factor that robs life of its meaning. Speed is often regarded as a supreme sign of vitality, but it is playing with death."[2] "Faster is better" might well be the motto of the age, but Sabbath helps us ask the question, "What price, speed?" and find the answer. The oil of Sabbath rest stills the stormy waters of our frenzied life.

We are desperately in need of a remedial course in deferment, waiting, stillness, patience, slowness. Cornelius Verhoeven, in *The Philosophy of Wonder*, writes that we have much to learn from the musical concept of the sustained pause, the *ritardando*. The *ritardando* is to music what the Sabbath is to the soul.

> The *ritardando* is the tempo of the man who has time and has nothing to fear from the closeness of things. A movement which slows down puts the mover to the test; it confronts him with a multiplicity of things at one and the same time. Slowness is a voluntary crisis in which the moving object focuses its attention and sums up in the one moment of slowness the road it has traveled and all that it has passed on the way. Slowness collects things. Not speed but slowness creates a link between things. Speed draws only arbitrary dotted lines which are soon forgotten. It destroys unity, isolates things, and creates distance.[3]

Erased, as we rush past all the *realities* that beckon, are the connections between them; between us and them. We have no time to wonder—to encounter reality as a "You"—when we race past people, natural wonders, needs, the Blessed Sacrament as disconnected "Its."

That the pause, the rest, is essential to the creation of rhythm, melody and harmony in music suggests its importance to the soul.

1. Cornelius Verhoeven, *The Philosophy of Wonder*, Mary Foran, trans. (New York, NY: Macmillan, 1972).
2. Ibid.
3. Ibid.

The Sabbath prohibitions against the use of speeding vehicles and productive machinery derive from the scriptural injunction to kindle no flame upon the Sabbath (Ex. 35:2). Abraham Heschel suggests that we must also beware the unholy fire of anger. The hostility of haste, of competition and envy, of rage against those who frustrate our progress or demand our patience, can be put to rest by Sabbath-keeping. The destructive flame will finally give place to the life-giving, creative fire of Spirit which we might otherwise have quenched.

We are in the world, but not of it; on the way, but not there yet; being perfected, but far from perfect; longing for eternity, but rooted in time. This quality of "betweenness" is characteristic of the human person and of the Sabbath itself. Sunday is just another day, shared by all regardless of belief; yet it is, for us, also a day outside the bounds of time. It gives us a taste of an eternal leisure and then returns us to the world of work, making us more fit for both while we wait in this between-time. Contentment with the slow pace of "betweenness" is a condition necessary for wonder—the profoundly human response to reality.

We tend either to speed through the week, through life, never stopping to be deeply refreshed, or to stagnate, resisting the demands of living the life we've been given, bogged down in complacency. Speed is enslavement to the urgency of every demand that assails us, but the incapacity to respond to anything *but* urgency is no less a bondage. Sabbath practices can be a counterweight to the varieties of speed that contribute to the deformation of our souls. Before we may wait upon the Lord, welcoming Him to the innermost mansion of our souls, we must become still. Stillness of mind, of body, is almost impossible to achieve unless we temper the furious pace of our lives.

Technological progress has given us modes of transportation, communication and manufacture for which we can be genuinely thankful. Like fast food, however, speed in these areas has its drawbacks. Sabbath separation from the use of machines—a Jewish practice—can help us distance ourselves from the dehumanization that lies within these technologies like a seed of destruction. A ruthless efficiency, rooted in the sin of pragmatism that values only the end result (Is the sock made? Is the message received? Have I reached my destination?), is likely to care little for means, or to see persons *as* means to valuable ends.

Faster is not always better. With snail mail you receive personality—in handwriting, stationery, style, scent—and the tactile sense of presence that email cannot convey. A face-to-face visit brings human touch, person as place, time as a gift, to an even greater degree, though it is admittedly less efficient and may be downright impractical. Cars zip us to our destinations, but at the cost of the health benefits of walking, the experience of natural and neighborhood delights along the way, or the social fun afforded by ambling or biking together. Columnist Leonard Pitts, Jr. calls convenience a "time thief." Convenience foods, permanent press fabrics, self-propelled lawn mowers and such—sold with the "implicit promise" that they would give us more time "to read and chat, to paint or play the piano or just pause and sniff those darned roses" have given us less and now make us feel guilty for taking "old-fashioned" time to do anything in a leisurely way. "Woe unto the unstructured moment . . . the moment you spend just being . . . we had more of them when life was less convenient."[4]

We are warned in Scripture of the dangers of witchcraft, of magic. "Wicca," from the same root in "wicked," meaning "to bend," is a use of power to bend and shape the natural world for our own purposes. C. S. Lewis was fond of demonstrating to his students that the word "technology" is more accurately paired with "magic" than with the word "science." If, on Sundays, we refrain somewhat from manipulating, changing, using the created world as means to our ends, we will, in some measure, slow down the race toward the tyranny of technology that exacerbates our lust for power. Let Sabbath be one day, at least, that you practice an inefficient humanity.

C. S. Lewis, Madeleine L'Engle and John Milton have all portrayed angels as existing at such vast speeds that humans can only perceive them if they slow down a great deal. The image of angels speeding along with the Milky Way and slowing to enter a timeless *kairos*, the moment of eternity where we can all be present to God and to each

4. Leonard Pitts, Jr., "Convenience a Time Thief," *Miami Herald*, 11-18-03.

other, is a fascinating parallel to our Sabbath observance. Somehow, it is consoling to think that perhaps the angels might also need to learn to be still and quiet and to wait upon the Lord.

Stagnation—inability to move forward or to make effort to attain spiritual goods—may afflict persons characterized either by constant, distracting movement, or by debilitating paralysis. Both prevent true engagement with whatever Reality is present to you in the present moment. For either expression of acedia, the Sabbath practices of slowing down are tonic. Moving prayer such as the Stations of the Cross, a pilgrimage journey to a nearby shrine, or a maze meditation might be just the symbolic stimulus you need to awaken your soul from deadly apathy. For help slowing down, think of the infinite patience of Christ, waiting in the tabernacle for your visit, waiting for the slow growth of His Body and the full coming of His Kingdom; waiting for His Bride until she can be perfected. In Him there is no haste, no hurry, no violence at all.

6 – Be Still

What I am can only be received by the other who gives me his full
attention, who is present to me and becomes aware of what I am,
and that I am good and worthwhile. The other who wills his
awareness of me opens his consciousness to my being,
and comes to know, that is, possess my goodness.
Conrad Baars, "Born Only Once"

I F IT IS DIFFICULT to begin to be slower, it may be doubly difficult
to actually stop and be still. At the root of this difficulty is a disintegration of body and mind caused by our racing past self, and
violating self in our haste to use our minds and bodies as means to
accomplish end results. Paradoxically, stimulation of body or mind
may be the way to reintegrate and still the soul. If your mind is
engaged, your body will relax its demand for constant motion.
Conversely, if you would relax and still mental churning, it will help
to engage the body. By "engaged," I do not mean "distracted," or
"put to work," but rather "focused attentively" in a way that promotes a restfulness of your whole, embodied self.

The great difference between amusement (literally, "non-think-
ing"), which increases the atrophy and lassitude of the soul, and
attention, which promotes a rallying of its faculties, is this quality of
intentionality, engagement, of listening alertness. Let's first see how
you might cultivate this quality physically, so as to still and quiet the
mind. Sports can take on the tone of driven, competitive, distracting
antagonism to holy leisure that characterizes popular culture. They
can also help build community, restore interior balance, help integrate body with mind, and promote the joy of Sabbath if these are
the intentions by which we gauge our participation. Only you can
discern whether physical recreations are resulting in the sort of true
interior relaxation we want to cultivate on the Sabbath. If sports
involvements destroy Sabbath community-building, present obsta-

cles to your presence at Mass, or cause increased tension between family members, you may want to save them for other days.

Other kinds of physical effort can be tremendously relaxing. Working in the garden, hiking, biking, beach combing, and the like can all become opportunities for family time, thoughtful engagement with nature, even prayer. More and more popular, as the negative repercussions of faster, more percussive, higher impact exercise are realized, such slow, intentional methods promote a listening attitude toward the body's needs and the messages it is sending through pain, stricture, energy imbalance and postural misalignment. "Labor is a craft, but perfect rest is an art. It is the result of an accord of body, mind and imagination."[1]

A simple practice of stillness is just to sit—whether in adoration of the Lord, or in quiet attention to what others need to say. Sitting is so obvious as to be easily forgotten. It is sometimes all we can do just to get our bodies to be still, sitting in one place for any length of time, resisting multi-tasking. Attention to aural or visual stimulation can help. Physical practice that increases balance, alignment, and deep relaxation will also help us learn to sit still. What we are cultivating, by all these practices, is a spiritual equanimity that enables us to "go with the flow," "roll with the punches," and "ride out the storms" of life. Recognition of the intimate mind-body connection and cultivation of self-aware mental quietude is central to all these forms of physical practice. Perhaps you will experiment with them only on a few leisurely Sundays, but the benefits will likely draw you to them more often.

Some form of physical prayer engagement, such as the rosary, or the Stations of the Cross, is common in Catholic and non-Catholic cultures—engaging the body, soul and mind together. Prayed only on Sundays, the rosary is a treasure; prayed at other times it becomes an oasis of Sabbath rest during the week. Conscious relaxation of the body—breathing deeply and focusing the mind slowly upon each part of the body, or upon each point of tension—is another way of bringing profoundly restful integration to body and

---

1. Abraham Joshua Heschel, *The Sabbath: Its Meaning for Modern Man* (New York, NY: Farrar, Strauss and Giroux, 1951).

soul. Finally, we have already seen that practices which help awaken the senses promote this mental-physical integration, quietude and attentiveness.

The faculties of hearing and of sight have particular power to foster the engagement of the mind that can bring restful stillness to the body. The listening ear is actually mind focused upon what is audible, or on imagined sound. Just listening attentively without an inward demand that response be made is very calming. A good conversation (and reading a good book is a form of conversation, when you are alone) keeps your body still far longer than you might otherwise stay. Listening to music might or might not also be helpful.

Much of what is called music today lacks the ability to be integrative, stilling, calming to your soul. Andrew Pudewa, in *The Effect of Music on Life*, details a scientific investigation into the effects of different types of music upon the brains of mice. The experiment had to be redesigned when the group of mice listening to heavy metal music began to fight and kill each other! Once the mice were all in separate cages, they were exposed either to the noise of heavy metal, or to the music of Mozart. Dissection of their brains, post-exposure, revealed either asymmetrical, ragged, disconnected neurons (metal), or symmetrical, graceful, beautifully linked neurons (Mozart, of course).

Other studies have demonstrated that music with a hard, driving beat drives up blood pressure and feelings of agitation and aggression. If you can't "connect" except to music like this, the key is to begin with it, but gradually to "step down" to more calming music. And integrative, calming music is not necessarily slow or boring. In fact, the selections that have been popularized as the stimulus for genius and creativity in *The Mozart Effect*, are "effective" because they are highly complex, rich and lively—fully engaging the mind rather than simply stimulating the pulse. Whenever you stop to spend time really listening to such music (not just hearing it as a backdrop to other activity) you will be giving yourself a Sabbath moment.

Just as the listening mind can promote the stillness and integrity characteristic of Sabbath rest, the seeing mind—the eye and mind engaged attentively together—also has this capacity to still one's whole being. When the ear hears words, the left brain—verbal, ana-lytical—is primarily stimulated. The faculties of reason, of logic are engaged to process what is thus received. What the eye sees, how-ever, is processed primarily in the brain's non-verbal, visual, sym-bolic right side. (Interestingly, the "Mozart Effect" of classical music seems to lie in the ability of such music to stimulate both sides of the brain and promote greater integration between them.) The bypassing of the rational, verbal faculty by visual reception gives a special appeal to such stimulation. Especially for those who tend to be dominated by verbal, logical thinking, or who must use it all during the week for purposes of work or study, visual means of engaging the mind may be the most relaxing and integrating to the soul seeking Shabbat Shalom.

The eye is designed to attend to movement, to change. It may have been over-stimulated by television to the point that it cannot rest its gaze upon images that do not constantly shift. A slow wean-ing may be necessary from visual "noise" as it was from aural noise. The capacity of television to manipulate the eye must be considered here. Not just another technology from which we might abstain on Sabbath as a link to slower, more humane rhythms of life, television is a particularly soul-deadening form of mind-numbing disengage-ment from God, others, real life, spirit. It is almost the antithesis of Sabbath rest. Let's explore why it has such power, and why your Sabbath design might well include leaving the TV off.

Return to the design of the eye. What stimulates the eye to attend is movement. The mind can also direct the eye to attend wherever you will, but it responds on its own to movement. The television industry, creating wealth by keeping you glued to the set for the advertisers who fund it, has long known the power of "visual events" to keep and hold your attention. A visual event is any change in focus, any movement of the camera, which has become your eye and manipulates what your brain will see. The more visual events per minute, the greater the hold of the screen over your eye, your attention.

Attention, thus dulled by mindless, meaningless events, needs ever-greater numbers-per-minute to maintain engagement with the media. Compare the rapid visual changes in current programming to shows even from the 1960s, or the visual frenzy of today's commercials to those of even ten years ago to see what I mean. The "plug-in drug"[2] is giving ever-higher doses to an addicted audience. One frenetic Japanese cartoon sent hundreds of children to hospitals having seizures—brain storms similar to epileptic fits. Perhaps their brains were, sadly for them, still actually engaged at speeds impossible to sustain and had not yet become dulled enough to endure the overdose.

Alternatives to this nightmare are the attractive visual delights of nature, an art museum, a movie that lifts the soul to beauty, truth, or holiness. Your Sabbath practice might include a nature walk with a magnifying glass, looking at art prints or museum books, or enjoying family photo albums for a visual feast that can include the loving closeness of persons. Drawing can be tremendously relaxing, and the eye that gazes upon a person to render his portrait has given him place in the heart of the artist. Sunday may be the only time you feel you have time to enjoy sketching or painting.

Praying with icons is another alternative. An icon can be, is meant to be, a profound encounter with God—an entering-in to the prayer of the iconographer and to the visual "word" given him by God. "The art of the icon catches the gaze of God in a way that no other expression, whether by word or image, could possibly do. A whole world opens, a world which reveals God's utter strangeness and yet simultaneously his immediacy, his vulnerability."[3] It frustrates the eye that seeks completeness on the two-dimensional surface, but grants entrance to the person who can be still and let the Spirit quicken the visual plane into a mystical moment of Sabbath peace.

We are learning to value *being* over *doing*—not just mentally, but in our conscious actions and self-restraint from acting. The Sabbath rest from productivity, haste, noise, and distraction helps us to be alone, to develop contentment with the fact that we are each, essentially, alone in this interior, still space. Henri Nouwen suggests that

2. Marie Winn, *Unplugging the Plug-in Drug: Television, Computers, and Family Life* (New York, NY: Penguin, 1977).
3. Esther de Waal, *Lost in Wonder* (Collegeville, MN: Liturgical Press, 2003).

the spiritual journey from loneliness to solitude is possible by "gentle and persistent efforts" and creates a fruitful "garden of solitude" where there was once a barren "desert of loneliness."

> The movement from loneliness to solitude should lead to a gradual conversion from an anxious reaction to a loving response. Loneliness leads to quick, often spastic, reactions which make us prisoners of our constantly changing world. But in solitude of heart we can listen to the events of the hour, the day, and the year and slowly "formulate," give form to, a response that is really our own. In solitude we can pay careful attention to the world and search for an honest response.[4]

Thus, all your acts of conscious stillness, slowness, and attention during the week prepare your soul to receive and to respond to the peace of Sunday. The ebb and flow of Sabbath and the week into one another creates a gentle, rocking movement that restores spiritual acuity to souls made dull by speed. The genuinely restorative rest of holy leisure awakens your soul and sensitizes it to the violations of mindless entertainments and frenzied fun. You will be amazed as you discover what self-defenses it has taken to endure them, and blessed as you release those defenses that have hardened your soul against the life of Christ within.

Think of Christ ever present in the tabernacles of our churches. With what perfect stillness He attends to you, waits upon you to hear His word of healing, listens to your cry for help! With what patience He waits to give Himself wholly to you at first opportunity! He is the example to your soul of a perfect poise between stillness and movement, listening and responding.

4. Henri Nouwen, *Reaching Out* (Garden City, NY: Doubleday & Company, 1975).

7 – Be in Community

The glory which thou hast given me I have given to them, that they may be one even as we are one, I in them and thou in me, that they may become perfectly one, so that the world may know that thou hast sent me and hast loved them even as thou hast loved me.
Jesus Christ, John 17:22–23

W E HAVE SEEN how the poverty of our own *being* leads to dispossession—the loss of self—and displacement—shutting out our fellow man. Has there ever been a time when so many people were more estranged from self, from God, from others? Alienation could well be the defining characteristic of the post-modern world. The solitude that Sabbath helps make of our essential aloneness—the capacity to be at leisure within one's own being, to encounter Reality from within that still, quiet center, to simply *be*—is the key to true community.

Until we possess ourselves we cannot give the gift of self; until you inhabit this still center where you may be "at home" with and present to yourself, you are "displaced" and hardly able to receive another. If our lives seem to be speeding out of control, our days passing us before we turn the calendar page, our relationships run like giant games of "Tag—You're It!", we must move inward to the still Sabbath center to recover our humanity and our sanity. Speed destroys unity. It is worthwhile to repeat this slowly. Unity—the integrity, the knit-togetherness of body and soul, of family members, of Christ and His Church—depends upon the Sabbath-aided development of leisurely, unhurried attitudes toward our lives.

If the human person is to hear the small sound of God's voice, to be sound in mind and body, and to resound the Word into the world, he must first have place, be contained. The vibration of a string in a vacuum does not become audible sound. That man is a harmony, that Truth is a symphony, implies emplacement—spatial boundary, actual material limits, location. From within such a chamber, *being* vibrates, resounds, gives voice to its identity and thus is known.

Until I hear who I am—the substance of place allowing me to hear my self, recalling me to myself—I am not fully *me*. I begin in a tiny womb, enter the wider womb of family life, and discover my expanding self further in the gothic interior spaciousness of the Church and in the many people who give me place within themselves. The unique qualities of each place, each person reflect me somewhat differently, molding the contours of my own soul. It has its own being, but is affected by, shaped by whatever, whoever else is planted there. Fear, ugliness, noise, haste, violence, and sin contract it. Trust, beauty, quietude, patience, love and virtue increase its capacity.

See the Sabbath just once more—the vessel God created, bounded by time and space, within which He Himself simply rested, was still, and had His *being*. From the beginning, He chose to make for Himself a tabernacle in this world, to condescend to its limits so that "I AM"—the very pulse of all life, the heartbeat of creation—could resound in it. No wonder that the desert tabernacle He designed was patterned after the pageant of Creation, that it culminated in the Holy of Holies—His dwelling place. No wonder His chosen people were, above all other signs of their identity, Sabbath-keepers. No wonder that Word came through Woman, handmaid to Queen Sabbath. And no wonder that Lord Sabbaoth sent the Spirit to make within each of us and in His Church tabernacles of His Presence.

Sabbath is, to the Eucharistic Lord, what your body is to your soul: its echo chamber, the space within which His voice—the ever-healing, ever-true, ever-creating Word—reverberates, is multiplied and magnified and goes forth. The Church exists within it; the family; the smaller lay and religious community; the individual; the world, if it only knew. If one of these voices, these beings, is tuned to, resonates with, the sound of Sabbath, its uniqueness blends in to the symphony of creation, of truth, without being silenced or violated or suppressed in any way. This is the phenomenon of the "both-and" of unity in diversity. "The Sabbath, thus, is more than an armistice, more than an interlude; it is a profound conscious

46

harmony of man and the world, a sympathy for all things and a participation in the spirit that unites what is below and what is above. All that is divine in the world is brought into union with God. This is Sabbath and the true happiness of the universe."[1]

The greater unity, integrity, a-tune-ment exists within self, family, community, the greater the sound of the "I AM." Not only do its vibrations nudge us toward effortless entrainment, lure us into the comfort and beauty of resonance with it, but we also can consciously seek to adjust ourselves into harmonious relation with it. Stuart Isacoff's *Temperament* describes the fascinating history of the development of piano tuning—from the early days in which each octave on each piano might sound just enough different to completely frustrate the transfer of a musical Idea from one person or place to another, to today's taken-for-granted, even-tempered keyboard that has enabled universal participation in the music of the world, transcending space and time.

There is a place for mathematical precision (let us hope the designers of airplanes value it, for instance), but in music—based upon intricate vibratory ratios, numerical patterns and intervals—mathematical precision gave way to the human person and to community. Pure Ideal worked its way through the imperfections, obstructions and subjectivity of the human being to become a somewhat imperfect Reality in which humanity could share. Such is the process by which, in Sabbath-keeping, we are constantly retuning ourselves to the Holy Sound and then carrying it out to the world in even the dullest-sounding pots of clay. To adjust our own note to its perfection, we must *be*, must sound out our own note, however dissonant, however embarrassing, so that our inner ear can direct our movement toward the one eternal Voice. To love Him is to sing with Him.

All community, whether religious or not, small or large, consists, then, in the degree to which it is in unity, in resonance with the "I AM," the Truth. Chiara Lubich, foundress of the Focolare Movement, speaks of "Christ forsaken"—that moment when Christ, still

1. Abraham Joshua Heschel, *The Sabbath: Its Meaning for Modern Man* (New York, NY: Farrar, Strauss and Giroux, 1951).

barely alive, abandoned Himself to the Father, then ceased to utter sound—as the key to unity, the *crucial* characteristic (literally, the quality of being crucified with Christ) of community. Jesus Forsaken shows us "that I am myself not when I close myself off from the other, but when I give myself, when out of love I am lost in the other." Each community thus multiplies the one, living, whole Church, not by splintering it but by freely uniting with it.

Father Luigi Giussani, founder of the Communion and Liberation Movement, describes this process: "What the Church is for all men is Jesus Christ's self-communication to the world. In this sense, what do five or six Christians meeting in a house represent? They connote the same thing: Jesus Christ, who communicates himself to the world through that ambit. . . . This means obedience to the total Church, depending on it, organizing one's life according to its rhythms, seeing oneself reflected in the other factors within the sphere of Christian life. These are aspects which define the validity of gathering together. Otherwise, what gives value to our coming together is not the mystery of Jesus Christ who communicates himself to history and the world, but something that has diminished its import."[2]

Every practice of solidarity—with family members, co-workers, Church authorities, for instance—understood in this light, is a Sabbath practice. Each moment of conscious identification with the Lord, forsaken on the Cross, and of subordinating self to others, or sacrificing self-interest for the sake of unity has the capacity to immerse our souls in Sabbath rest. Much of the unrest, the weariness of life can be attributed to the constant struggle to have our own way, to hold ourselves aloof from the needs of others, to maintain self without recourse to other human beings or to God. When we lay all this at the foot of the Cross, we are refreshed and renewed. When our families bear this mark of unity, home becomes the Domestic Church. "The Church thus finds in the family, born from the sacrament, the cradle and the setting in which she can enter the

2. Fr. Luigi Giussani, *Why the Church?* (Canada: McGill-Queen's University Press, 2001).

human generations and where these in their turn can enter the Church."[3]

As we choose our actual Sunday practices, we employ conscious gestures—doing or non-doing—to help attune ourselves to this note of unity. The constant refrain of the Jewish people—often the last note sounded by Jewish martyrs—has been, "Hear, O Israel, the Lord your God is *One!*" On Sundays, if you will seek ways to honor and cultivate the indivisibility of the Eternal One, you will echo His precious, chosen people into whose family you have been grafted. Read aloud the Gospel passage (John 17) in which Jesus prays for the unity of His people. Take one car at one time to church instead of attending in shifts. Choose one single mission, or country, or charity to pray for. Resist kindling the fire of anger within your family, or introducing any form of division. Sing together at home and let liturgical music take on a new significance. Give one away of something you have two of. Write one letter or thank-you note. Pick one person in your family to secretly bless somehow. One is the number of "identity"—multiplied by one, every other number is itself. Let the number ONE resound on your Sabbath and in your life.

It once was a given that shared meals were at the heart of unity, of community life. The first Christians, in addition to sharing the Lord's Day Bread, spent time eating and sharing lives together. Sadly, we can no longer take for granted that the home table prepares souls for the Eucharist and resounds its call to communion throughout the week. Carl Honore's *In Praise of Slowness* contrasts the nutrition-deficient fast food industry with the small, but steadily growing, "slow food" movement. Eric Schlosser's *Fast Food Nation* chronicles the parallel developments of faster cars, speedier highways, and the idea of fast, impersonal food for busy, isolated individuals.

Gone are the nightly family dinners of yesteryear, says Robert Putnam in *Bowling Alone* (a fascinating study of the components of "cultural capital" and the indicators of its decline). In their place we have every-man-for-himself, short-order, micro-waved meals-in-minutes, and fast "food" eaten on the run, or in the middle of traf-

3. Pope St. John Paul II, *Familiaris Consortio*, Paragraph 15.

fic. The table has lost its significance as a place of family unity, the kitchen its role as a place where creation and love and food and time are woven together to create true sustenance. Speed has broken the bonds forged by sharing ordinary meals and families are atomized into near-nothingness.

With the loss of shared meals we have lost a great deal of conviviality—shared life. Lack of time for the appreciation, selection and preparation of food has led to decrease in our capacity to value what is good about food and about eating itself. Instead of feasting with family on real, beautiful, nourishing foods that heighten our appreciation of companions, of life, and of the Eucharistic meal, we feed at public troughs of pseudo-food—chemical lies and poisons extruded in mouth-titillating variety and served to us by people conformed as much as possible to the images of the "food service" machines they operate like robots. Eating is, instead of respite for the soul and a symbol of Sabbath, a necessary function to be performed as efficiently as possible so as not to interfere with our busy lives. Is it any wonder, then, that, thus debased, we approach the table of the Lord as an obligatory intrusion into the one day we want to use for a long list of other activities?

Or, perhaps, we have come, with a Manichean duality, to the place where we feel pride in our utilitarian, minimalist approach to food. Eschewing wine and beauty and luxurious expense of time and effort, we practice a joyless asceticism—unbroken by Sabbath feasting—that leaves us unable to enter into the goodness, messiness, sensuality and camaraderie of creation. Do we also say, nobility on our brow, "thanks, but no thanks" to the feast of graces and means of grace prepared for us at the banqueting table of God?

The movie *Babette's Feast* is a beautiful response to this feast-less-ness of our lives. Make a long, slow, beautiful meal a part of your Sabbath, and your appreciation for *slow* and for one another will increase. If this meal also makes time for the kind of thoughtful, lingering conversation that builds genuine friendship, then it will help prepare your soul for friendship with God. In the Eucharist we are invited, as a community, to the banqueting table of the Lord, where He has prepared a feast for us in the midst of our enemies. Sabbath is a reminder to see a meal as a sacrament.

8 – Be Not Afraid

The works that have really grown from the loving work of men, from mind and heart and hands, work into which a man's own life has passed, give not only that man's life to the world for ever, but one more visible sign to man of his image and likeness to God.
Caryll Houselander, "The Reed of God"

"B E NOT AFRAID"—probably the most-quoted phrase of Pope St. John Paul II's pontificate, and his legacy especially to the youth who flocked to hear him. Human beings are meant to thrive, not just to survive; to enter the abundant life Christ makes possible, not to commit suicide. Sabbath principles have implications for economics, environmental stewardship, social justice, labor relations, the arts, health—every area of human endeavor and concern. The only agent powerful and small enough to carry them into every nook and cranny is *you*!

Our goal cannot be an earthly utopia, but neither can we wish away the world by ignoring it out of existence. Christ will create a new heavens and a new earth in His own good time. This one will end catastrophically, through the processes and events of history, and persons will survive—embodied souls will still exist when everything we call "culture" has collapsed. "[T]he end of Time, within history, will be a downfall, a catastrophe. Nonetheless, [man's] attitude to history, his attitude to the future may not be one of despair."[1] Christians, on the contrary, can possess the virtue of hope "that renders the believer able and willing to act here and now, within history, indeed even to see in the midst of the catastrophe itself a possibility of meaningful action within history."[2]

---

1. Josef Pieper, *The End of Time* (Fort Collins, CO: Ignatius Press, 1999).
2. Ibid.

"Freedom from illusion not only does not contradict hope"[3] but confirms it.

No one knows how close we are to the end of time, but anyone can see the barrenness, misery, confusion, evil and brokenness of today's culture. There is no doubt that we will be tempted to lose hope, to be afraid, but Sabbath keeps us from the abyss of despair. There is a *via media* between the extremes of selfish striving against others in a desperate struggle to survive, and of cringing in panic, shrinking from life itself. That narrow road is hope. We have seen that Sabbath corresponds to the human quality of "betweenness," of knowing we do not yet fully know. In this sense, Sabbath corresponds also to wonder—the flame of spirit that lights up the man and lights the world up for him. The essential qualities of Sabbath—stillness, quietude, cessation from self-assertion, freedom from the tyranny of the urgent—are prerequisites to the state of wonder in which man is most fully aware, awake, alive—most human. The structure of wonder—the ability to *be* in the "between," or "on the way," to know without fully grasping—is the structure of hope.[4] Keeping a holy Sabbath cultivates in us the virtue—the power to be human—of hope.

The hopeful man, with no utopian illusions, no denial of his own limitations and weakness, is the very one to invest himself in the welfare of the world for the sake of souls who may be brought into the Ark before the end of time. The image here is of a robust and potent (man-ly, *vir*ile, human potency that is neither male, nor female) personhood fully engaged with life and literally, actually, transforming the world by his way of seeing it and his way of *being* in it. Some of this transforming *being* of his will be public, overt, visible, but much more will be hidden, interior, infinitely small. He is ready to live, ready to die. "[O]nly the man who combines in himself this affirmation and this readiness will retain the possibility of historical activity, arising out of a genuine inner impulse."[5] In other words, the locus of control—of his will—is deeply, authentically,

3. Ibid.
4. Ibid.
5. Ibid.

interior, in contrast to the people we see all around us who, living egocentrically, in effect give this control, their free will, into the keeping of any peer, expert, celebrity or dictator who catches their attention or self-interest.

Though huge numbers of people and imposing institutions are arrayed against the individual, free, human person, he has a power greater in its small scope than all their destructive power. The man of virtue, of holiness, of wholeness can create a genuinely new thing—a thing which itself has reproductive power, the power to multiply what it *is*. When you see the converse—the essential impotence of unholy persons—you will not be as tempted to fear their flailings or despair at your own smallness. As Sabbath begins to turn the upside-down world right-side-up for you, this perspective will dawn on your consciousness. Philosophy, wonder, is "the highest or at least the most intense form of life. To think is to be involved in life to the very verge of one's identity. It is the boldest venture man can undertake and proof of considerable vitality."[6]

Whatever you do in genuine freedom will, to some extent, be countercultural—a stand taken against a culture that devalues life, disrespects its elders, debases the gift of human sexuality and "democratizes" brilliance into a mire of mediocrity. Even a feast is a revolution! "Every time in history that men and women have been able to respond to the events of their world as an occasion to change their hearts, an inexhaustible source of generosity and new life has been opened, offering hope far beyond the limits of human prediction."[7]

At your Sabbath feast, on your Sabbath walk, during your prayers, in your visits and letters, through your works of art, speak of the hope that is in you! Encourage others, and determine to slay needless fears that interfere with your enjoyment of life. Sabbath is to be a delight—especially to cultivate delight in reality. Contemplation, our greatest need, involves "taking a long, loving look at the

6. Cornelius Verhoeven, *The Philosophy of Wonder*, Mary Foran, trans. (New York, NY: Macmillan, 1972).

7. Henri Nouwen, *Reaching Out* (Garden City, NY: Doubleday & Company, 1975).

real."[8] Don't let anything rob you of that treasure. For one day, whatever your station in life, whatever your level of education, be a philosopher. Take time to ponder on and wonder at the design of the human person; read an encyclical; study the Catechism; celebrate the courageous contributions of the saints in history; spend time in the bold venture of thought!

Cultivate courage and hope by the Sabbath practice of contemplating the Sabbath itself. Keep a keen edge on your awareness of the ways you are practicing Sabbath-keeping and the effects you are experiencing. Discipline yourself to think of no other day, but to remain intensely, intentionally present to the whole Sabbath day. Ask yourself who needs your encouragement, your infusion of this hope Sabbath is giving you. Ask Christ to help you be fully present to Him in the Eucharist as He is fully present to you.

8. Fr. William McNamara, "Holy Leisure" (A Taped Address).

Conclusion to Part II

When you hearken to the voice of the Lord, your God, all these bless-
ings will come upon you and overwhelm you.
Deuteronomy 28:2

B Y NOW you could fill a book yourself with ideas of ways to
consciously set Sabbath apart, to prevent its profanation, to
enjoy its profound rest and to proclaim its counter-cultural
message of hope. In Part III you will go on to deepen your understanding of Sabbath, and then to explore in Part IV some of the further implications of the idea. Meanwhile, you will be in the midst of
knowing it by lived experience. If you are committed to letting Sabbath have its way with your soul, these different ways of knowing it
will more fully form the idea into a reality within you.

Great ideas are lost on us unless we choose ways of enacting
them, making them real through actual embodiment, or expression. All the practices I have given are merely suggestions of ways
you might consciously slow down, be more quiet and attentive,
interact with the beauty of saints, creation, or works of art; ways to
cultivate the qualities of human *being* and to cultivate true community, starting on Sundays. Our Sabbath practices are intended to
help Christ's presence permeate every day and every sphere of our
lives. Setting aside a special day that is centered in worship is the
best way to achieve the deep restfulness that will diffuse, like the
smell of perfume, through your week.

Though it is true to say that there will be as many expressions of
Sabbath-keeping as there are believers, six common threads of
human personhood run through all the suggestions I have made.
Sabbath calls us to, and helps us attain, the *via media* between seemingly opposite extremes of unrestedness. Though we may be more
comfortable with the familiarity of behavior unbalanced toward
these extremes (after all, we can stay *there* in our own strength!), we

are kept mindful by Sabbath of the narrow road where we must have Christ's constant grace to keep us in equanimity. This is not the balance of a static object, inert once it has "arrived," but the dynamic balance of a living person—a constantly growing and changing Reality.

Instead of a distracting busyness, or an indolence indifferent to spiritual goods, Sabbath offers us a place of interior encounter with our own *being* and with Christ. Instead of deafening noise or crushing silence, Sabbath cultivates within us an expectant, listening quietude. When we would speed through time, or remain spiritually paralyzed, Sabbath invites us into the slow dance of wonder and leaves us poised to act, or refrain from action, gracefully. In a world of mindless, uncreative, surreal amusements and frenzied, restless fun, Sabbath calls us to true, recreative, refreshing leisure that is mindful and aware of the Source of our humanity. As opposed to our avoidance of others through isolation or crowd-seeking, Sabbath helps us form and sustain true community and friendship. When we are tempted to brace and harden ourselves for survival, or to succumb to panic, Sabbath breathes courage and hopefulness into our souls.

Ultimately, your consciousness of the meaning of Sabbath and its implications for the wholeness, the holiness, of the human person will find many other expressions through your rested, enlarged, enriched soul. You become, for the world, for others, what Sabbath has been for you—a refuge, a place of encounter with the Lord of Love, a welcoming home. You also become a sign of contradiction— someone whose life points the world away from its focus on everything but God, and toward the only source of genuine restoration.

Sabbath teaches you to be attuned to God's voice, to your own unique needs and calling, to the hearts of the people around you, to the wonders of creation, to beauty wherever it may be found, and to Truth you can't help but proclaim. By more closely aligning you with Christ—Lord of the Sabbath—she helps you become more like Him, and thus more human. It may take some extra work during the week to keep Sunday spacious and free of work, or some careful planning to fill Sunday with just those things that restore and renew the light of Christ in your home and soul. You may have to trust

God with the results of laying down your work, your projects, you advancement for a full day each week.

When you commit to setting apart a Sabbath rest from activities that draw you away from interior serenity, you cultivate your soul's capacity to receive more of the grace of God. The more deeply you grow to value stillness, quietude, beauty, communion, virtue, the more you will grasp the value of this priceless gift. Gradually, you will realize why Sabbath is the key to personal, familial and cultural restoration and peace. Awareness and understanding dawn as practice begins, and your practice will grow more authentic and natural as the light brightens. In the vessel of time kept turning by the graceful hand of Queen Shabbat, your soul is shaped to the contours of eternity by its Lover.

The Jews understood Sabbath as the point of balance in the week and in the person. "The right balance between the light of *hesed* (grace) and the fire of *gebura* (power), between the fire of creativity and the light of the awareness that we are ourselves created and kept alive by God, is the secret of the good life in the eyes of the Torah."[1] The candle flames that welcomed in the Jewish Shabbat also symbolized the extra soul given to each person on the Holy Day to help and transform his soul. The transforming, creative fire of the Spirit of God was given special place on Sabbaths freed of man's own creative work. In our Christian Sabbath-keeping, in our interior quietude, journey becomes pilgrimage, waiting becomes hope, silence becomes listening, suffering becomes healing in every Sabbath moment. And so, the world is transformed.

1. Abraham Joshua Heschel, *The Sabbath: Its Meaning for Modern Man* (New York, NY: Farrar, Strauss and Giroux, 1951).

PART III
Established by Understanding

*Happy is the man who finds wisdom, and the man who gets under-
standing, for the gain from it is better than gain
from silver and its profit better than gold.*
Proverbs 3:13

*Picture yourself on the roof beam of a house under construction.
From your perch you can look down and see, instead of separate
rooms, the whole floor plan; instead of blueprints, the three dimensional structure. If you have been putting into practice the idea of
Sabbath, you realize that your knowing-by-experience will never be
complete, will never exhaust the riches of Shabbat Shalom. Yet I ask
you to more firmly establish your growing apprehension of the idea
by learning more of Sabbath's history and its correspondence to the
human person. To know by intellect what one has known by trust,
and by experience, is to more fully possess and integrate the many
dimensions of the object of knowing. As you read the next two chapters, your experience of Sabbath will be enriched by deeper understanding of its symbolism and potential.*

9 – Roots of the Tree of Life

Beloved, come to meet the bride; beloved, come to greet Shabbat.
Enter in peace, O crown of your husband; enter in gladness,
enter in joy. Come to the people that keeps its faith.
Enter, O Bride! Enter, O Bride!
(from "L'cha Dodi", sung to
welcome the Sabbath)

T HE ROOTS of a Christian understanding of Sabbath lie deep within our Jewish heritage. Observance of the Sabbath, according to ancient rabbis, "outweighs all other commandments,"[1] marks the Jew as one of the chosen people, and reveals an individual's essential quality. In calling himself Lord of the Sabbath,[2] Jesus directs us to the profound Jewish understanding of Shabbat as a basis for comprehending His own identity. For thousands of years, Jewish scholars have explored the symbolism and meaning of the gift of Sabbath. A Christian "day of worship" disconnected from these riches is a pale, weak thing indeed.

Originating in God's own example of taking a day of rest at the culmination of the world's creation, and obedient to His command to "keep the Sabbath holy,"[3] Jewish observance of the Sabbath is first and foremost an act of worship, of glorifying God. Nothing that God created, though it was good, was *holy*. Only the seventh day, that day upon which God created "rest," possessed the quality of holiness. This "rest"—in Hebrew, *menuha*—"is the same as happiness and

---

1. Pinchas Peli, *Shabbat Shalom: A Renewed Encounter with the Sabbath* (B'nai B'rith Center for Jewish Identity, 1988).

2. Luke 6:5, "And he said to them, 'The Son of man is lord of the sabbath.'" (RSV)

3. Deut. 5:12, "Observe the sabbath day and keep it holy, as the Lord your God commanded you." (RSV)

stillness, as peace and harmony."[4] Our Good Shepherd, we are told, leads us "beside the still waters,"[5] "the waters of *menuhot*."[6] And weekly, the Jews have followed Him, laying down the cares and duties of this world to honor and encounter the Lord of eternity. *Menuha* became synonymous with eternal life.[7]

Far from being a mere symbol of eternity, the Sabbath is an actual emergence of eternity into the dimension of time. "If eternity means the combined simultaneous experience of all three tenses of time—past, present and future—then by celebrating the Sabbath we are able to experience eternity every week. We find ourselves in accord with the heartbeat of all time, as conceived in the Judaic vision of the universe."[8] As rabbis searched the Torah for wisdom, a two-fold response to God's sanctification of the Sabbath emerged in Jewish practice. In Exodus, we are told to "remember" the Sabbath, and in Deuteronomy, to "observe" or "keep" the Sabbath (Ex. 20:8, Deut. 5:12). Jews thus sanctify, or set apart, the day of rest both by prescribed prayers and practices, and by abstention from certain activities.

Like the positive image and the negative space composing a work of art, the remembrance and observance of Shabbat recreated within the people of Israel the tabernacle of the very Presence of God. In prayers and traditional practices, Jewish families recalled the Creation, their exodus from slavery in Egypt, and their hope of ultimate salvation in the person of the Messiah. "[W]hen the Sabbath is entering the world, man is touched by a moment of actual redemption, as if for a moment the spirit of the Messiah moved over the face of the earth."[9]

By their restraint from activities associated with creative work—shaping and using the material world—Jews made of the Sabbath an "island of rest." The idea of sacred space, holy places, had been

4. Abraham Joshua Heschel, *The Sabbath: Its Meaning for Modern Man* (New York, NY: Farrar, Strauss and Giroux, 1951).

5. Psalm 23, "He leads me beside still waters; he restores my soul." (RSV)

6. Heschel, *The Sabbath*.

7. Ibid.

8. Peli, *Shabbat Shalom*.

9. Heschel, op. cit.

manifest in earlier cultures, but the chosen people introduced the concept of sacred time to a world accustomed to constant toil for material survival. "The idea that a seventh part of our lives may be experienced as paradise is a scandal to the pagans and a revelation to the Jews."[10]

The specific activities designated by the rabbis as forbidden were derived from the thirty-nine categories of work involved in making the desert Sanctuary of God. Though we are likely to feel overly constrained by long lists of such work as cooking, sewing, tilling fields, and repairing equipment, the Jew was freed by them for the perfect, "fortieth work" of cultivating his soul for heaven. "Unless one learns how to relish the taste of Sabbath while still in this world, unless one is initiated in the appreciation of eternal life, one will be unable to enjoy the taste of eternity in the world to come."[11]

The Sabbath prohibitions against the use of speeding vehicles and productive machinery derive from the scriptural injunction to kindle no flame upon the Sabbath (Ex. 35:2). Abraham Heschel suggests that we must also beware the "fire" of anger. If there are activities we feel we have no choice but to engage in on the Sabbath, we have the opportunity to transform them into gifts given freely to others, or into prayers of willing suffering. Such transformation is a high calling of the fully human life, and both honors the holiness of the Sabbath and prevents us from ruining our rest with grudging.

Not only are we called to fellowship with one another as we pursue conversation and community in the delightful context of Sabbath rest. There is also a sense in which we "enter into fellowship with the day."[12] Sabbath is a holy guest to be greeted, a bride to be praised and loved. Israel was told by God that Sabbath would be its spouse. "The Hebrew word *le-kadesh*, to sanctify, means . . . to consecrate a woman, to betroth."[13] The association of Sabbath with womanhood—queen, or bride—signifies "majesty tempered with

10. Ibid.
11. Ibid.
12. Ibid.
13. Ibid.

mercy"[14] and corresponds to woman's role as the place (womb, matrix) for the development of people. By lighting the Sabbath candles each Friday evening, a Jewish woman sanctifies her self and her home, and prays for the blessings of Shabbat Shalom upon her family and the world. "[T]he sacred space that had been the Temple transformed the sacred time of Shabbat, and the sacred time of Shabbat transformed the home into sacred space."[15]

The hope of the Messiah is central to the Jewish sense of the Sabbath. In the kingdom of the Savior, Israel would finally be wed to its beloved Shabbat, and the people of God would enter His own restful, joyful, eternal peace. Mary, the Mother of God, embodies the holiness—the wholeness, purity and perfect freedom—of the soul wholly consecrated to her Lord. Patient, receptive to the creative Will, empty of self-seeking—the Chosen Vessel fulfilled *in her being* the purpose of the Sabbath rest. The day—sanctified and sanctifying; queen and crowning glory of creation; conforming all within her to her own dimensionality; multiplying within time and space the open vessels of the spark of Spirit. The Woman—utterly receptive to the formation of the Son of Man within her; made by God His meeting place and gracious hostess to His guests; Queen of Heaven drawing all men toward Christ through the vast hospitality of her own soul. Jewish Sabbath-keepers were intimately prepared to receive Messiah of the Sabbath—Jesus, Son of Mary.

Adrienne von Speyr gives a beautiful image of the way a person becomes *place* by the kind of quiet surrender and attentiveness to God that occurs for us during Sabbath rest: Mary "has senses like every person, but she does not use them as other people do, to adorn herself, to win something for herself and make it her own. Instead of closing off her senses for herself, she opens them up for God; she uses them only to serve a better comprehension of the divine will, to its greater honor and glorification. She surrenders to God the purpose and end of every act of her senses. So her senses are an open space in which God can manifest himself at any time;

14. Ibid.

15. Francine Klagsbrun, *The Fourth Commandment: Remember the Sabbath Day* (New York, NY: Random House/Harmony, 2002).

they are ready for the angel."[16] Our senses, freed by Sabbath from distraction, develop greater capacity to receive the blessings and meaning of the material world. Even this pleasure can be given to God in imitation of Mary, so that each gift received through our senses becomes a praise of His glory.

Mary not only models for us, but also invites us in to her own heart to be conformed to the shape of a soul wholly receptive to her Son and to all those He calls to Himself. Though her heart was grievously pierced by sinful man, she yet opened her soul to the crucifying world and gave birth to His Church in forgiving love. Though the Sabbath takes us, in its way, out of the world, it, too, returns us better prepared to redeem it. The Sabbath-keeping soul is an open place—an open wound at times—in which the needy are invited to find safety, rest, hope and love: encounter with Lord Sabbaoth. "Rest therefore acquires a sacred value: the faithful are called to rest not only as God rested, but to rest in the Lord, bringing the entire creation to him, in praise and thanksgiving, intimate as a child and friendly as a spouse."[17] Mary is the bridge between Old Covenant and New, the spring in the desert, the place where eternity entered time in the person of Christ. Sabbath corresponds to her in a special way, as a vessel of heaven on earth.

The first Christians, aware that they constituted the "fulfillment of the Hebrew people phenomenon,"[18] chose to celebrate the resurrection of Christ on Sundays. Creation returned to life by the atoning death of her Savior, death itself vanquished by the Cross, and the bearers of God's image released from bondage to sin—the fullness of their "eighth day" joy could not be overstated. On one hand, they sought to differentiate themselves from the Jews, and on the other, to demonstrate Christ's fulfillment of Jewish law and Messianic prophecy. The Christian Sabbath, while released from the Talmudic prescriptions and proscriptions, was yet a day set apart as holy, holy,

16. Adrienne von Speyr, *Handmaid of the Lord*, E.A. Nelson, trans. (San Francisco, CA: Ignatius Press, 1985).

17. Pope St. John Paul II, *Dies Domine*, Paragraph 16.

18. Fr. Luigi Giussani, *Why the Church?* (Canada: McGill-Queen's University Press, 2001).

holy by a people destined for eternity. The pagan "day of the sun" was thus invested with Christian meaning, linked to the stories of creation and redemption, and imbued with the life-giving light of Truth.

The Lord's Day, as the Sunday Sabbath was called, became an "*Easter* which returns week by week."[19] From this pivot-point in time, one looked back upon salvation history: the preparation of the nation through which the Messianic hopes of the world would be fulfilled—a people prepared by Sabbath observance to receive the Lord of the Sabbath; through the agony of the crucifixion to the final, earth-shattering silence of the sealed tomb. And from this point the first Christians looked triumphantly forward from the New Day which had dawned upon the world on the Sunday of the Risen Lord toward the world's own rebirth. The kingdom had come, was daily coming, and at His next appearance would perfectly have come into the hurting, longing world through their very beings as the Eucharist made of His Church His Body. Holy, indeed, was this new day, and set apart for the worship and praise of God!

Just as Sabbath spaciousness lifts idea into form, time into space, Woman into Tabernacle, person into open channel of grace and Church into Body and Ark, so it makes of all Sabbath symbols sacred signs—true carriers of the spark of spirit by which the material world is revivified and returned to its noble task of resounding the Creator's praise. Each woman, each candle, each humble loaf of bread, each smell, each act of self-restraint, each moment of silence becomes pregnant with the Shekinah, the glory of God, and gives birth to His Spirit in the world of men. Jewish tradition holds that by the Sabbath the world is en-souled, receives anew in the pause that will become eternity, that fullness God intended for it from the beginning. Though we may not adopt each aspect of the Hebrew practice, our own design of Sabbath can be informed, enriched by this heritage of signs.

At the Jewish Sabbath meal, two loaves of bread recall the double portion of manna collected in the wilderness by the people of Israel on the sixth day in preparation for rest from labor on the holy sev-

19. Pope St. John Paul II, *Dies Domine*, Paragraph 1.

enth day (Ex. 16:5). The connection of Sabbath with manna reminds us that both Divine Providence and our obedience sustain us, and that our own hearts affect what we can receive from God. Each person gathered only as much as he could eat. None could be retained for the next day—a reminder that grace is not available to us now for an imaginary future moment—lest it become foul (Ex. 16:20). On the Jewish Sabbath three feasts are eaten—abundance, indeed—in honor of the threefold use of the word "today" in the Sabbath commandment (Ex. 16:25). Again manna reminds us that the present day is the day of grace. The Sabbath prohibition even against gathering for the day reminds us that God most fully fills the empty vessel that humbly waits upon Him.

The finest foods are reserved for Shabbat. Wine is blessed in overflowing cups and passed around for a sharing that presages Christian communion. "Simple white candles usher in the day and a colorful twisted candle escorts it out; the one announcing the stoppage of all creative activity, the other its beginning again."[20] The very letters that make up the Hebrew words "Shabbat Shalom" carry complex significance—linking the Sabbath to the ideas of Mother, Water, Home, High Tower, Great Connector, Learning, Teaching, and the very Name of God. Through Sabbath, the Torah connects the Tabernacle to Creation. "The connection between Shabbat, shrine, and cosmos reveals itself in part through a mysterious scheme of sevens within the Tabernacle texts."[21] The Tabernacle is thought to be a type, or pattern, of the created world. The holy of holies where He makes His dwelling place corresponds to Sabbath, to Mary, to the Church, and to the heart of the Christian.

Creation, liberation from slavery, marriage, home making, God's faithfulness and sovereignty, and unity among the chosen people are all celebrated and cultivated by Jewish Sabbath prayers and Scripture readings. A place is left empty for Elijah, who is said to arrive at the dining table at Sabbath's end to announce the Messiah's arrival. The coming of the New Elijah, the Savior, is expected to usher in the era of eternal Shabbat Shalom. The signs of Sabbath are

20. Klagsbrun, *The Fourth Commandment.*
21. Ibid.

so much more than symbols—so full of meaning and so powerful to convey that meaning. How much greater are the Sacraments by which actual realities are conveyed by signs full of these high Ideas! Behold, the Sunday Sabbath: St. Augustine calls it a "Sacrament of Easter."[22] Not only does it *remind* us of the resurrection, but it also actually *conveys* into our beings—as individuals and as communities—the Bread of Heaven, the new life of the Risen Christ in His own Body and Blood. The Eucharist is then the pinnacle of Christian Sabbath observance and the source of its manifold blessings to us and to the world through us.

It is no wonder that Pope St. John Paul II exhorted all Christians to "rediscover Sunday.... The rediscovery of this day is a grace which we must implore, not only so that we may live the demands of faith to the full, but also so that we may respond concretely to the deepest human yearnings."[23] Christ Himself, in His tomb, brought forth from this seemingly lifeless "Sabbath rest" a new day and a new meaning for all Jewish practices. The Sabbath precept of the first covenant "prepares for the Sunday of the new and eternal covenant."[24] Recognizing the fact that God has set it within the Ten Commandments, "Israel and then the Church declare that they consider it not just a matter of community religious discipline, but *a defining and indelible expression of our relationship with God.*"[25]

The fact that Christians are no longer bound by Talmudic law to specific Sabbath practices should in no way imply that the commandment to remember the Sabbath and keep it holy has been repealed. The commandments form the "basic structure of ethics"[26] for humanity and, as such, confirm the Scripture's teaching that "the Sabbath was made for man" (Mark 2:27). If we can first believe that God's laws are designed to bless us, and then that Christ came "not to abolish but to fulfill the law" (Matt. 5:17), we can make room in our minds for the idea that Sabbath rest and Sabbath sanctification

---

22. Pope St. John Paul II, *Dies Domine*, Paragraph 19.
23. Ibid., Paragraph 7.
24. Ibid., Paragraph 8.
25. Ibid., Paragraph 13.
26. Ibid.

of time are the loving and wise prescriptions of a Great Physician—
"meant to prosper and not to harm" us (Jer. 29:11).

The task of the sacrament of Easter is to convey actual participation in the Passion, Entombment, and Resurrection of Christ. This
threefold pattern gives us another way to think more deeply about
the meaning we want to convey, the reality we hope to embody, and
the story we want to rehearse by the practices we adopt. Sanctification by separation becomes, in the new covenant, sanctification by
identification with Christ. We might think of the Friday, the Saturday, and the Sunday of the fulfilled or Messianic Sabbath as aspects
of Sabbath to embrace on each of the three days, or in different Sunday practices.

Friday reminds us of the value of suffering, of being passionately,
utterly spent on behalf of the world Jesus loves and draws to Himself. The Jews took care to serve and provide for the poor on Fridays
before the Sabbath candles were lit. The implication for us might be
a greater awareness that our tiring week of work can be offered as a
gift to Christ, or our sufferings united to His. We might choose Friday as a day for particular acts of self-emptying, in preparation for
the Sabbath torrent to come, or make works of mercy the "Friday"
aspect of our Sunday practice. Christ has become our model for
Sabbath observance, and His self-sacrifice was, for Him and thus
for us, the necessary precursor to fullness of Sabbath joy.

The silent stillness of Saturday's tomb turns our thoughts to
Christ's cessation of His earthly work, to Mary as she carried the
developing Child, and to the souls in hades who received Christ
prior to the Resurrection. With the Jews, we might refrain from creation, from imposing our self and from expanding our hold on created things. Allowing time for solitude, interior emptiness, silence
in union with "Christ Waiting" shapes this aspect of our Sabbath
observance. Devotion to Mary, prayer for the souls in purgatory,
and particular attention to the needs of the unborn and expectant
mothers all echo the "Saturday" aspect of our Sabbath.

The primary "Sunday" characteristic of our Sabbath-keeping
should be the joy of the Resurrection and communion with Our
Lord. Christ created a Church to make *place* for us to meet with
Him—He who would never leave us or forsake us—as a body, His

Body. God does exceedingly, abundantly more than all we can ask or imagine (Eph. 3:20). The Jew expected to serve and to obey the Messiah when He arrived, but never imagined he would be called upon to bear His Body, Blood, Soul and Divinity within his own person! Prophecies prepared Jews for a suffering Savior, but nothing except encounter with Christ can prepare anyone to be crucified with Him—to die to self to make place within for Him to dwell. That we work and recognize the sacredness of space is a function of our existence as creatures. That we rest and recognize the sacredness of time is a function of our Jewish heritage. That we co-create and recognize the sacredness of persons is a function of the Good News of the Risen Lord.

Pope Benedict XVI, in his closing homily at the May, 2005 National Eucharistic Congress in Bari, Italy, emphasized our need to rediscover the Sunday Eucharist as a source of vital energy for Christian living in a world "often characterized by rampant consumerism, religious indifference, and secularism closed to transcendence."[27] The Holy Father echoed the words of Pope St. John Paul II who, in his encyclical *Dies Domine*, said our Christian hope will be "renewed and nourished by this intense weekly rhythm."[28]

The Catholic Catechism tells us that our day of rest should provide for a respite from everyday work and give others a rest from theirs.[29] Sunday is a "protest against the servitude of work and the worship of money."[30] It is "a time for reflection, silence, cultivation of the mind, and meditation which furthers the growth of the Christian interior life."[31] "On Sundays . . . the faithful are to refrain from engaging in work or activities that hinder the worship owed to God, the joy proper to the Lord's Day, the performance of the works of mercy, and the appropriate relaxation of mind and body."[32] Marty Barrack, author of *Second Exodus*, suggests "[S]unday Mass,

27. Pope Benedict XVI, May, 2005 Address to the National Eucharistic Congress, Bari, Italy.

28. Pope St. John Paul II, *Dies Domine*, Paragraph 38.

29. *Catechism of the Catholic Church* (New York, NY: Doubleday, 1994), 2187.

30. Ibid., 2172.

31. Ibid., 2186.

32. Ibid., 2185.

followed by a family Rosary, followed by a family lunch filled with conversation about the priest's homily, or the Scripture readings. Then maybe a Catholic movie such as 'Jesus of Nazareth,' 'A.D.,' 'Babette's Feast', or . . . 'The Miracle of Marcelino.'"[33] Parents might also want to include Bible or Catechism lessons for their children.

All the doing and non-doing of our Sabbath practices—the ways of attachment and of detachment—help us to remain poised between time and eternity as open channels of grace into the world. For the Christian, the "eighth day" is an order of magnitude greater even than the entire week of seven days—a supernatural fullness of time that overflows all existing boundaries of time. Perhaps because of this quality of boundlessness, it is difficult to design our Sabbath practice.

On the one hand, Christian doctrine does not demand common observances beyond the Eucharist. On the other, it is impossible to imagine any structure, design or program of practices sufficient to contain the infinitude of meaning inherent in Queen Sabbath, now that she has welcomed her Incarnate King. If Sabbath is to be kept, as obviously I think it should, it cannot be kept in submission to law, but only as a creative response to the Resurrection. It is this very response-ability that is cultivated in us by every intentional act, or non-action with which we set apart the Sabbath to keep it holy.

Whatever symbols we incorporate into our Sabbath-keeping, let them begin in *value*. That is, let us first be filled with wonder at the power of the Spirit to quicken symbol into sign, and sign into Sacrament. Then let us learn that what we value, we multiply into the world and set ourselves the task of valuing what Queen Sabbath teaches are the highest things: Communion, peace, leisure that elevates and forms the soul, quietude that invites the Lover of our souls to speak, marital love, the goodness and beauty of created things, mercy, hospitality and above all, praise to God. We *make* the Sabbath holy, just as we *make* love—by embracing and responding to the Beloved. We delight just in being together, with no particular purpose in mind, no rush, no desire except to give the unimpeded gift of self and to receive the Other wholly.

---

33. Marty Barrack, in personal correspondence.

Let us make of our Sabbath a time of opening our senses to God: the aroma and taste of festal foods, the candlelight that softens and transforms our view of those we take for granted, the beauty of our home's order and cleanliness, the thrill of truly beautiful music. From ancient times, Jewish practices have affirmed the goodness of creation by such Sabbath appeals to the senses of man—inviting his complete surrender to the good, pleasing and perfect will of the Creator. We have seen how this intuitive response of the Jews in linking taste, texture, smell, sound, and beauty to Sabbath practice has the effect of heightening the soul's capacity to receive reality. How appropriate it was to help prepare a people for the Reality of the Savior.

At each Sabbath's close, Jews say goodbye to her in the prayers of Havdallah—passing around sweet spices so everyone may inhale and symbolically retain the fragrance of Shabbat in the coming week. Christians carry away from Sabbath in their persons the fullness of the Eucharistic feast—the candlelight that dispels all darkness, the echoes of common prayer and sacred music, the interior spaciousness of souls turned and turned again on the wheel of liturgy, and the sweet smells of sanctifying incense. The "cathedral" of Sabbath becomes inward reality through surrender of our senses, of our embodied souls, to rest. Amen, let it be so.

10 – The Sabbath Person

Think through me, thoughts of God, My Father,
Quiet me till in Thy holy presence, hushed,
I think Thy thoughts with Thee.
Amy Carmichael, "Gold Cord"

I PROMISED we would move from the understanding of Sabbath's historical development to an understanding of its potential. Sabbath not only *has* potentiality ("the ability to develop or come into existence") it also *is potentia*, a power to make potent the human person. Sloth is, in contrast, in every sense an impotence—a powerlessness, in the face of all that assails us, to value the goods of the Spirit in a way that causes the Spirit's fruits to be born in us, through us into the weary world. We have looked briefly at six facets of personhood—signal qualities of the human life lived abundantly, authentically in counterpoint to the dehumanizing pressures of the hostile world around us. Hopefully our Sabbath practices are, more and more, cultivating these qualities in us and in our homes. Because the seemingly insignificant changes you are beginning to see in your own being, your own small sphere, have such tremendous power to affect the world, I want to deepen your understanding of the awesome thing God has done in giving *you*—one free fully-human being—to the world.

Picture with me for just a moment, a person. He stands, feet firmly planted wide apart, arms lifted up and out toward the sky. See him poised joyfully, receptively, triumphantly between heaven and earth, between time and eternity, between the macrocosmic speed of dancing planets and the microcosmic speed of spinning atoms! Forming an "x" with his body, he reminds us that man is a multiplier and, literally, a crossroad—an intersection, a "between-ness." Created to know, to love, and to serve his Creator, he is commanded to go forth and multiply. His purpose is threefold and he exists, so to speak, in three planes: "above," "below," and in "between."

The fullness of Shabbat is better understood through the lens of personhood. Sabbath *is* the realm man reaches up to touch, the eternity in which his soul lives and moves and has being. Sabbath *is* the interior chamber, the now moment within the person where he may retreat into *kairos* at any time and encounter the Person of Christ. Sabbath *is* the Lord's Day rooted in the ordinary week, the simple, temporal pause from which the rhythm of the good life emerges to bless the created world through the Body of Christ. The threefold nature of the Sabbath—seen fully only through the Cross of Christ—corresponds so perfectly to the nature of the human being that we cannot help but believe that, truly, the Sabbath was made for man.

This human being, the bearer of the Divine image, whose brokenness wounds the world and whose restoration brings it healing and redemption, is the "stream in the desert," the channel of Living Water to a thirsty world. The Eucharistic Sabbath, the Resurrection Sunday, is the deep pool, the ocean of mercy where he must dwell so that it may dwell in him. We are reminded that man is the living link between that mercy and all who need it. If we would enter in to the fruitfulness implicit in the gift of Sabbath, we should delve into the threefold purpose of this person—the purposes God has promised to accomplish through him. We have seen ways in which Sabbath-keeping enriches the *quality* of being human. Let's look more deeply into Sabbath's correspondence with the *purpose* of our humanity.

It is easy to see how we might take advantage of the Sabbath to better know the Lord and one another. Worship itself is an act of the whole person in which we get to know, come to love, and offer service to the Lord. By receiving Him in the Eucharist, we know Him in the intimate sense of actual participation in His Body, Blood, Soul and Divinity. Jewish rabbis taught that, lest Sabbath rest be filled with intellectual labor and acquisition of new knowledge, "on Shabbat you read and study what you've already learned; you bring your own creativity and thoughts to your studies. This is the difference between being smart and being wise."[1] Our Sabbath cessation of directing and affecting the world around us helps free us from the pride that thinks we know all we need to know, and helps us cultivate a poverty of mind that is fertile ground for Wisdom. "To prepare ourselves for service we have to prepare ourselves for an articulate not knowing, a *docta ignorantia*, a learned ignorance.... In short, learned ignorance makes one able to receive the word from others and the Other with great attention. That is the poverty of mind."[2]

This capacity to "not know" is at the root of wonder—what St. Thomas Aquinas calls the desire for knowledge. Philosophy, the love of wisdom that characterizes the most fully *human* being, is "an obstinate ignorance," an avoidance of "certain knowledge."[3] It "takes its momentum [from] and finds its orientation" in theology.[4] Intimate knowledge of Christ "fully reveals man to himself"[5] and the life of Christ within man lights the fire of wonder—the active longing to know—from which philosophy springs. The capacity to know, to turn toward wisdom with docile receptivity, and toward the world in wonder is at the core of personhood—animals and angels do not possess it[6]—and so it flourishes in the Sabbath-rested soul.

To lose this capacity for wonder "means that someone takes one's immediate surroundings (the world determined by the immediate purposes of life) so "tightly" and "densely," as if bearing an ultimate value, that the things of experience no longer become transparent

---

1. Malka Drucker, *Shabbat: A Peaceful Island* (New York, NY: Holiday House, 1983).

2. Henri Nouwen, *Reaching Out* (Garden City, NY: Doubleday & Company, 1975).

3. Cornelius Verhoeven, *The Philosophy of Wonder*, Mary Foran, trans. (New York, NY: Macmillan, 1972).

4. Josef Pieper, "The Philosophical Act," in *Leisure, the Basis of Culture* (San Francisco, CA: Ignatius Press, 2001).

5. Second Vatican Council. Dogmatic Constitution on the Church in the Modern World, *Gaudium et Spes*, Paragraph 22.

6. Josef Pieper, "The Philosophical Act": "Ancient philosophy understood wonder as in fact the distinguishing feature of human existence. Absolute spirit does not experience wonder because the negative does not enter, because in God there is no ignorance. Only the one who cannot grasp something can feel wonder."

... whereas the one who experiences *wonder* is one who, astounded by the deeper aspect of the world, cannot hear the immediate demands of life—if even for a moment, that moment when he gazes on the astounding vision of the world."[7] Holy leisure, Sabbath rest, cultivates this intentional and temporary "deafness" to immediate demands that allows room within us for wonder. Only true leisure frees man from "the working world of the work-day, not through his uttermost exertion, but as in *withdrawal* from such exertion."[8]

St. Thomas Aquinas agreed with Aristotle that spiritual joy and wonder are inextricably linked—the capacity for one is capacity for the other. In this we are reminded of the joy Sabbath practice brings, and of the sheer delight in it that Sabbath-keepers experience. Take for your Sabbath practice the time to see in things around you their deepest meaning. "To contemplate things in wonder is to attribute to them an infinite significance."[9] Refrain, as much as possible, from the use of and transformation of things so you can be mindful of what they already *are*.

Look for inherent value that makes good things worth doing, even if badly. Let this be your guide: practicing great things in small ways is infinitely better than reducing great things to our smallness. Plan to truly stop and see one thing each Sunday. Gaze upon the human beings around you with awe—as upon vessels of glory, types of Christ, as beings already higher than the angels by virtue of yearning to know God and His creation!

Let things take your breath away as, at least on Sunday, you release yourself from the immediate demands of life. "Wonder at reality demands the humility to sit at the foot of a dandelion. The proud are so full of themselves that there is little room to marvel at anything else. Saints are typically awestruck at an insect, a flower, a star because they are burning with love and rooted in a perceiving honesty. That is, they are humble."[10] Slowly, quietly, be present in

---

7. Ibid.
8. Ibid.
9. Verhoeven, *The Philosophy of Wonder*.
10. Fr. Thomas Dubay, *The Evidential Power of Beauty* (San Francisco, CA: Ignatius Press, 1999).

the world, as an Adam or an Eve—fully, abundantly human, knowing and naming each thing you see. Speak into being, with God, the world around you, freshly each week. Bless it, as Sabbath blesses you, into being.

Acedia dampens the fire of our love for God, without which we cannot fulfill the very purpose of our creation. Sabbath rest breathes life into these embers as surely as oxygen rekindles life in a drowning man. It takes time to love—to so fully open the heart to another that he is given place, takes shape within your own being, and to be affected by and conformed to his being. We can "know" many things intellectually, but to love is a more whole reception, made possible by our wholeness. To know "on the basis of an inner correspondence"[11] is "to suffer," to share in, to be related to what Martin Buber would call a "You"—a fully dimensional Other with whom true encounter is possible. The movement from the scattered, disintegrated self toward the wholeness of being, of humanity, that makes love possible within us is the movement toward restoration of interior quietude, toward welcoming the Lord to take up His throne within us and conform us to Himself. This movement increases our capacity to love.

At first, when Sabbath-keeping is quite new to us, we suffer from the double-mindedness that Satan first cultivated in Eve—the double *being* (one a stark reality, the other an idea or image of self) that fights against the simplicity of soul characteristic of virtue. "Blessed are the single-hearted, for they shall enjoy much peace."[12] We may seem to be such strangers to ourselves that we have difficulty even "making place for," "being at home with," or loving our own beings. The grand image of self cannot condescend to welcome the pitiful reality. But little by little, as the Lord has His way in us, He heals and reconciles and expands our souls. The greatest thing we can do to facilitate this process is embrace the Sabbath rest He provides—to rest in Him utterly at least on the one day when we receive Him in His fullness. "Just as the removal of cataracts restores clear vision, so does repentance restore the joy of youth and a capacity for the

---

11. Pieper, "The Philosophical Act."
12. Thomas á Kempis, *The Imitation of Christ* (Chicago, IL: Moody Press, 1982).

beautiful."[13] We say, "Lord, I am not worthy to receive You, but only say the word and I shall be healed," and then the Word Himself enters and restores us in whatever measure we can receive Him.

As we move from Sabbath to Sabbath, growing in the capacity to love and to be loved, the qualities of Christ known as virtues are formed in us. From within a soul thus formed into His likeness begins to shine the beauty of holiness. Father Thomas Dubay likens this radiance to the dazzle of a symphony performance. "Just as a world-class symphony concert is an elegant and harmonious unity of dozens of instruments and thousands upon thousands of notes producing dazzling melodies, so also the tens of thousands of details in a virtuous human life synchronized by free will decisions and orchestrated by prudence are fired by love into the matchless beauty of holiness."[14]

We are freed by the Sabbath and its Sacrament to be fully human, fully alive. Having loved ourselves by giving ourselves this deep, healing rest, and by reconciling ourselves to the Truth spoken in love by Our Lord, we develop a spacious liberty to offer hospitality and love to others in His name. Sabbath is the perfect time to practice self-awareness and to develop loving rituals that nurture your own senses, body, mind and soul. Do not be afraid that by caring for yourself you will become selfish. Take the long fragrant bath, the nap, the walk in the woods.

Have the great feast with champagne and the best dishes, if only for your self, or welcome others to share your growing Sabbath joy in a slow meal. The task of holiness is simple, in a way—just to be whole. Speeding ahead of your self, multiplying activities without regard to the needs of your body, refusing to stop and listen to what your pains are trying to tell you, depriving yourself of true food, community and beauty—all are disengagements from the task of holiness; refusals to treat yourself as a human being full of majesty and set apart for noble purposes. We are commanded to love others as ourselves, and cannot fully turn toward them until we

13. Dubay, *The Evidential Power of Beauty.*
14. Ibid.

have embraced our own *being* with a sense of the value God places upon it—with love.

Among the many teachings of Pope St. John Paul II is his consistent affirmation of the observation, in *Gaudium et Spes*, that "man ... cannot fully find himself except through a sincere gift of himself."[15] We cannot be fulfilled, fully human, without transcending the confines of our own selves. In a very real way, a person's *being* is, literally, born ("borne" also, as a weighty load is borne) in those who love him, who give him place in their hearts. Christ Himself condescended to the estate of man and even now is being born in, borne by us. We have the ability, the noble duty, as humans, to serve one another by growing in wholeness, in holiness. Not only does our virtue light the way for others, but it also provides a way for their own "becoming." Thus is the Body of Christ—His Church, the Person of Our Lord—made whole and given *being* in our midst. "God breaks up the private life of His saints and makes it a thoroughfare for the world on the one hand and for Himself on the other."[16]

I suggest especially that you find ways to place the lives of saints in view on Sundays (read a biography, look at a photo or icon, ask for their prayers, visit a shrine, tell someone their story). "The life of holiness, resplendent in so many of the People of God, humble and often unseen, constitutes the simplest and most attractive way to perceive the beauty of truth, the liberating face of God's love, and the value of unconditional fidelity to all of the Lord's law, even in the most difficult situations."[17] Of course, the more your acquaintance with the saints permeates your daily life, the more power they will have to draw you, attract you toward virtue (which is, literally, "the power to be human").

Created to be knowers, lovers and servers, people go about their lives knowing, loving and serving, to some degree, whether or not

15. Second Vatican Council. Dogmatic Constitution on the Church in the Modern World, *Gaudium et Spes*, Paragraph 24.

16. Oswald Chambers, *My Utmost for His Highest* (New York, NY: Dodd, Mead, 1935).

17. Pope St. John Paul II, *Veritatis Splendor*, Paragraph 107.

they are believers in God. The question of their wholeness, their humanity, their fulfillment of God's intentions, has more to do with the *objects* of their very human exercise of these capacities. Whether truth is known, or lies; whether goodness is loved, or evil; whether beauty is served, or mammon—these distinctions are more to the point. In this sense, one of the greatest benefits to be reaped from Sabbath is to have our gaze redirected on a regular basis to worthy objects of the application of these human faculties.

Many of the Sabbath practices already recommended have in mind this "weekly tune up" of our focus—upon God Himself, upon truths, upon reality as mediated to us through our senses and awakening us to its Creator, and upon beauty and creativity as expressions of solidarity with His own wondrous mind. Meditation on the lives of saints, contemplation of Holy Scripture, development of higher tastes in literature or music, all have in common the intentional direction of our interior gaze to "whatever is true, whatever is honorable, whatever is just, whatever is gracious, . . . excellent . . . worthy of praise" (Phil 4:8). In this way, the Sabbath helps us learn not only to be content and present in the present moment, with the reality we encounter here and now, but also to continually reach for higher things, *best* things. In this sense we cultivate a holy dissatisfaction with reality insofar as it does not correspond to truth, goodness, and beauty.

The objects of our lingering gaze—those things we contemplate and value—form our souls and also become the very things we multiply into the world. In this sense, we reach downward into the third plane of our existence, to reproduce what is in us so that another person may share it. Man the "multiplier" is able to give himself to those around him by placing something of his own being into forms in which they can receive it. Those beneath him in age, stature, strength, wisdom, or capability may only be able to receive some small portion of all that is his to give, but he is responsible—able to respond—to serve them with his whole being. He has power, virtue, to take everything he has of knowledge, love, talent, truth, understanding—everything of self—and somehow make it accessible to others. In loving condescension—literally, coming down with others—he makes of himself a feast for those around him. In this, he is very like Christ, who made Himself as nothing in order to feed the world His own Body. Through him the portions of self others are able to give into his keeping are multiplied as he receives them in their full significance, with a heart of wonder. Their needs move through his own heart in prayer that begins the formation of the response God will make through him.

This fully human person finds within himself a drive to re-present—Christ to the world, the needy to God, the beauty of nature in a painting, the Idea of Sabbath in the form of practice, Idea into Form. One yearning of love is to know the object of love more fully, and another is to re-present whoever or whatever we love. When we have known, have gazed—upon the Lord, a saint, a spouse, a natural wonder, a Grand Idea, or, in fact, upon any thing that is, that has being . . . on a Reality, a "You"—the object takes form within us and our love for it grows until we desire to respond by some form of secondary creation.

Whatever we create—a drawing, a verbal description, a life like theirs, a poem—is somehow unable to convey the full dimensionality of the original; it is necessarily reduced, or flattened. But in the attempt is a very real multiplying that is uniquely human. One way of many in which we are made more whole by the gift of self is this creative response to whatever we "possess" inwardly. For, as we give the creation out into the world, we give a window by which others may also gaze upon the object of our attention. The Holy Spirit quickens the representation into life within those who receive it. Thus, others may enter in to the blessedness of our experience of love, or truth, or beauty.

In Sabbath, God gave man such a window—a day from within which he could see through to eternity, to the glory of the Lord—could direct his gaze in wonder at the entire creation and find God represented there. In the Sabbath people, Israel, God restored the clarity of the window, which man had turned into a mirror, and in her the Jews could see, could wait upon expectantly, could quietly trust in, the coming Savior. In the Eucharistic, threefold Sabbath, God has given Christ, the window through which man can see himself fully known, fully loved, restored, and whole. In the Sabbath-keeper, He has given a window through which the world may see

Christ. You, a single human being, have the capacity to be such a window to the extent you align yourself, restore yourself with Sabbath's gifts. The actual, conscious, growing practice of Sabbath is the key to the reclamation of the human capacity to know, to love, and to serve God and humanity.

The Jews believed they could tell the essential qualities of a man by his Sabbath-keeping. Pope St. John Paul II believed the person's authenticity is revealed by his action, by what overflows from his heart into the world. What he multiplies is what he truly is. What he represents, recreates in the world shows what he loves. Contrary to the teachings of modern, rationalist philosophers, the most authentic person is not the most powerful, but is the one who manifests this interior integrity and uses his will to pursue good—the individual bearer of Christ. "Only Christ-bearers can restore the world to life and give humanity back the vitality of love."[18] The Sabbath rest strengthens the still core of authenticity, keeps us poised between our yieldedness to God and our wielding of self in the world. It strengthens us against servile conformity to the dehumanizing ways of the world and against the apathy and indifference at the other extreme—the two forms of inauthenticity Pope St. John Paul II observed. It comes down to this: shall we continue to multiply frenzy, distraction, noise, insanity to poison the world, or shall we enter the Sabbath rest of God and begin to multiply peace?

18. Caryll Houselander, *The Reed of God* (Allen, TX: Christian Classics, Division of Resources for Christian Living, no date shown).

PART IV
Treasure-Filled Knowledge

The teacher must entrust to God, to the mystery of Being, to that
Measure which made us and which we cannot measure, which
exceeds us in every way—must entrust to him alone the
ever wider spaces that the surprising paths of the pupil's
freedom opens up in his dialogue with the universe.
Fr. Luigi Giussani, "The Risk of Education"

With each Eucharist, each day of holy leisure, each intention and
practice, you are knowing Sabbath with the wholeness of your being.
To know as a human person is to dwell richly with the object of
knowing, to the extent that the fullest possible dimensionality of that
object is reproduced within you. This is the way we are known in
Christ, and in Him live, move and have being. His Incarnation
showed us our own—our human—capacity to give Him being.

As we return, through Sabbath, to the full estate of our humanity,
we discover that there is such a close correspondence between Sab-
bath and the human person that they cannot be understood apart
from one another. Pope St. John Paul II told us that the world desper-
ately needs for us to continually "recapitulate the human person"—
to say, to show, over and over what a person really is, and to perceive
that this—this personhood, this re-presentation of God's image and
substance, this calling of man back to wholeness—is the measure of
all the values and activities and institutions of man.

Now, either we have arrived at a place of "species arrogance," or at
a pivotal comprehension of the work and worth of the human being
in the world. Let's back up and approach this moment from the per-
spective of the historical development of the Sabbath and of the sense
of personhood. We have seen that the pagan mind was attuned to
"actuality"—to the whole cloth apprehension of "what is," received
poetically, experientially, as a child receives the world before his ver-
bal abstractions distance him from it. This childlike mind had a sense
of sacred space—an ability to differentiate and set apart certain

places in response to encounter with the Divine. In calling out Israel to become, as a people, sacred space—a vessel for His presence—God gave to personhood a greater dimensionality. The covenant that had embraced a person, a couple, a family, and then a tribe was now embracing a nation with the intention of blessing the world through it.

The Jewish mind was attuned by the Sabbath—sacred time, sacred cycles—to duality; to the utter "other-ness" of God, of His people and of the Seventh Day. The law kept them moving between the poles of self and alien, week and Sabbath, remembrance and expectation, rest and work, nature and supernature, eternity and time. The vessel, the keeping-place of the Word, was formed over time in the turnings. We must know something of the further dimensionality brought to personhood by the life, death, and resurrection of Christ if we are to understand what it means to be, ourselves, fully formed.

To a people prepared by sacred time to be a vessel, and to a woman so formed, came Christ. The capacity to receive, to know not just by trusting another or by the evidence of the senses, or by the operation of intellect, but to know by one's whole, integrated, surrendered being is—as we see in Mary's example—the capacity to receive Christ. The fullness of grace He is offering to each of us and to the Church is this capacity to let Him be fully formed in us and thus to bring the world to encounter with Him.

Thus, the Christian mind can be said to be attuned to creativity— to a holistic knowing of "what is" (an idea, a tree, a person, a truth) that is capable of re-presenting, re-producing it into the world to be received by other persons. The Jew, holding the tension of paradox within his very being through trust in God, was made ready to receive the Messiah—the resolution of all tension. The Christian (the Christ, the Church)—looking back and forth upon all history from the Cross—is, to the degree of his or her capacity to receive being from the hand of God, the creative resolution of the particular paradoxes or tensions that are met in his unique person. He is the place of transformation, the channel of grace. The world is made new and the kingdom comes in him.

I do not say that man himself has become some new thing, but that what he is has been revealed gradually to his own mind to restore him from a fallen state and return him to himself. If we would restore the capacity of man to receive other people—most importantly to receive the Person of Christ—as fully-dimensional realities, we must attend to what makes him fully human and challenge whatever compromises his dignity, freedom, and capacity to be human. We have looked at Sabbath through the lens of personhood, and now turn to look through the lens of Sabbath at the world around us. In the same sense as we turn from each Sabbath back toward life in the "real world," I now turn to three pairs of topics which expand our sense of the effect souls at rest may hope to have upon that world: restoration of our capacity to wait by revolution in our understanding of time; restoration of our capacity to help form souls by revolution in our understanding of education; and restoration of our capacity to evangelize by revolution in our understanding of the power of beauty.

11 – A Sabbath Sense of Time

Time is dead as long as it is being clicked off by little wheels,
only when the clock stops does time come to life.
William Faulkner, "The Sound and the Fury"

Man was commanded to be fruitful, to multiply. Since then, he has filled the world with the clutter of man-made objects and abdicated his role as steward of creation. He has, we have, largely lost the capacities for effective action, and for self-restraint—without which we are less human, less humane. We lack response-ability, the two-sided potential—for self-wielding and self-yielding—characteristic of the human being fully in possession of all his faculties, fully mature, fully virtuous. The Eucharistic Sabbath promises restoration of the human person and proclaims him in the Person of Christ and in our very beings. We are given to the hurting world to suffer with it and to act on its behalf.

Most of us want very much to be responsible for our share in the world; to help solve the world's problems; to have a positive impact during our short time on earth. But Sabbath asks us to undergo a revolutionary upheaval in our relationship to time: to learn to waste it, to pour it out as a thank-offering; to return some of it to Him in trust.[1]

Time is, from the human perspective, both the matrix, the structure, within which we grow and develop, and the resource entrusted to our careful stewardship. Sabbath rest helps us make peace with the cyclical nature of time, and to balance our "use" of it with our discovery of our "placement" within it. The cycles of days, weeks, years, and seasons do more than mark the passing of time. They are the Author's "plot engine"—propelling the "story" forward toward

1. Fr. William McNamara, "Holy Leisure" (A Taped Address).

87

resolution. A useful analogy is a forest—both resource and place. If the trees remain unused, no home will be built, no fire will burn; whereas cutting down all the trees for lumber and firewood removes the forest's value as a place to call home. Sabbath is the weekly point of balance between time ordered to useful work and time ordered toward our place within God's story. The eighth day, more than large enough to counterbalance the weight of seven, is critical to our equanimity.

To ignore the need for work, or forward motion, is to be tossed and turned by the cycles of time (the feeling we have all had of being tumbled and turned and flattened by the next wave before we had a chance to accomplish anything). This corresponds to the extreme of indolence—the passivity of the person who cannot wield himself, for himself or for others. To ignore the cyclical nature of created time is to become a machine—trading rest and quality of life for the illusion of constant progress and forward motion. This attitude corresponds to the extreme of busyness which, as we have seen, also may characterize the slothful person. He lacks something of the capacity to yield his activity to the purposes of others, or to the purposes God has for him.

As its wheels turn within wheels, time takes shape—form mirrored in the development of the soul. Jews speak of an "architecture" of time—form generated by ritual, liturgy[2]—of Shabbat as a place of sanctuary and restoration for the soul and restoration of the broken vessel of God's glory. The entry of eternity into time has the effect of quickening symbol into sacrament, substance into sacred vessel, and person into place.

By helping us develop detachment from labor, concern for money, bending time and material to our own purposes, self-centeredness, haste, and isolation, the Sabbath shapes the soul into an empty vessel prepared to receive grace. We see negative space—silence, emptiness, rest—as a positive element in the composition of our lives, as it is in any work of art. Sabbath's role is, in part, to open the eyes of our heart to the beauty of time not marked for use—set

2. Abraham Joshua Heschel, *The Sabbath: Its Meaning for Modern Man* (New York, NY: Farrar, Strauss and Giroux, 1951).

aside for the action of God upon our soul, instead of for our action upon the world. Sabbath observance fights against acedia, against dullness, by returning our souls to fervent love of God. Acting as a "placeholder" in time for the presence of God, Sabbath makes of our hearts vessels which can receive His being; capacities into which He pours the torrent of His love.[3]

Another virtue that opposes itself to the erosion of our souls is patience. If we would transform the busy, restless, unthinking world around us, we must cultivate patience, and with it a supernatural sense of time. The waiting, the non-doing, the "triumph over diversions"[4] that characterize true patience are all cultivated by Sabbath observance. As we step to the center of the spinning disc of daily activity, we grow still. In true worship we are lifted from the impatient march of *chronos* into the eternal moment of *kairos* time. In cessation of activity, our souls are reawakened to the operation of the Divine Will upon them—to His loving discipline and still, small voice.

We experience, on our Easter-Sabbath, a taste of Christ's patience in allowing Himself to be acted upon, and of His victory in enduring the utter stillness of the tomb. "The self is both an actor and a reactor. [T]he story of Jesus Christ testified that this 'passive' side of selfhood lay at the very center of the secret of redemption."[5] Waiting patiently in the center of Sabbath eternity, our conception of time begins to be transformed.

We drop out, for a time, of the common practice of dizzy distraction that is both cause and result of a flattening of our souls. We gain a new perspective on the world of speed, size, money, power, amusement and manipulation. We become resensitized to the falsity of breaking time into homogenous boxes and forcing ourselves to fit inside them. We notice that time is more than a resource to be used. Sabbath makes us more and more aware that time is a created

3. Bl. Angela of Foligno: Christ said to her in a vision, "Make yourself a capacity, and I will make myself a torrent."

4. David Bailey Harned, *Patience: How We Wait Upon the World* (Boston, MA: Cowley Publications, 1997).

5. Ibid.

thing, that it can be sanctified, that our being transcends it. If time and space form a two-dimensional matrix within which our being unfolds, Sabbath can be said to add a third dimension, giving *being* the capacity to receive its fullness from the life-breath of the Spirit. By virtue of this gift of holy leisure, the soul is given a spaciousness, a resilience that resists the pull of time and the burden of space.

Sabbath frustrates our desire to control time, to identify only with our work and productivity. Sabbath teaches us to live in the moment—to be fully present to God and to others, to integrate mind, spirit, will and body in the expectant waiting upon God that is the essence of hope. This expectancy is illustrated in the Jewish celebration of Sabbath—awaited each week with longing and greeted with joy at each Friday evening entrance. Through Sabbath rest, we learn a new approach to time that involves trust in its Creator. Instead of using and manipulating time in a fruitless, selfish way to accomplish our own purposes, we find the seeds God has planted being birthed within us in the fullness of time. The change in us comes from within, organically, authentically, as we experience this intimate encounter with the Spirit.

Abraham Heschel, Jewish author of the classic text, *The Sabbath*, calls Shabbat "Spirit in the form of time." "Earlier generations of our human race, not ruled by alarm clocks, saw the hours personified, encountered them as messengers of eternity in the natural flow of time growing, blossoming, bearing fruit."[6] Ultimately, as we return week after week to this encounter, Sabbath permeates all other time with the sense of possibility, of limitlessness, of expectation. "[T]here is no 'now' on our clocks" but now is "the only place where we really *are*. . . . We are only real to the extent to which we are living in the present here and now."[7] We learn to release our hold on time, to trust the Lord with the resource of time, and to fully inhabit the moments we pass through instead of filling them with activity, or sleep-walking through them unconsciously.

As Sabbath revolutionizes our sense of time, and as we grow in patience—in capacity for waiting—we grow more capable of being

6. Heschel, *The Sabbath*.
7. Ibid.

content with the slow unfolding of our own being. The importance of Sabbath-keeping to the development of this capacity for waiting—on ourselves, on others, on the Lord—is worth exploring in further detail. First, let's see how the journey—a form of waiting—can be helpful in living out our commitment to holy leisure.

It may seem ironic, at first glance, to mention the journey as a practice of Sabbath rest, of counterbalancing the rapidity of life. After all, don't we travel at the high speeds we are trying to learn to do without? But a closer look at *journey*—a universal metaphor for the process, the living of life—reveals how it can teach us to wait. The enjoyment of travel is rarely had by those who are focused on destination. By all accounts, the deepest joy of the journey is the joy of process, and not of progress. In fact, whenever hastiness and goal orientation intrude into the trip, its delights are compromised.

Travel can be a form of retreat, of spiritual rest, and as such, lends itself to Sabbath practice. On a journey, we are detached, for a time, from both our starting point and our destination—suspended, in a way, in the present moment, the "now" which, like Shabbat, seems somehow outside normal time. "We are *en route* for the sake of what lies on the way, not in order to pass it but to possess it . . . the way is only . . . the fashion in which we take possession of it."[8] Speed flees from one point, or toward another and denies "all that lies between . . . all that is real."[9] The best journey is an immersion in the "between," a taking-possession of all that is most real in life.

When we travel, the normal demands of daily work are held somewhat in abeyance, if not entirely erased. We have permission, unless we bring our restlessness and addiction to distraction with us, to just *be* wherever we are. "Going with the flow" becomes a way of life as we meet whatever challenges arise with inner equanimity. And when (of course!) that equanimity is disturbed, we have the time just sitting in cars, on trains, in tents, on mountains, or in museums and castles, to recover—if we have given ourselves a travel schedule that respects the need for such spaciousness in time.

8. Cornelius Verhoeven, *The Philosophy of Wonder*, Mary Foran, trans. (New York, NY: Macmillan, 1972).
   9. Ibid.

Journey can be, like the Sabbath, a pilgrimage—an encounter with the divine in sacred spaces, holy places, moments of insight and wonder. We bring our selves to the journey, as we do to the Sabbath. All our baggage, physical and emotional, burdens us and we yearn to be freer of it, to lighten the load more and more as we go on. We may be humbled by finally being the alien and, pushed or pulled out of the comfort zones of shared language and culture, become newly conscious of what it means to be human. On the journey we are not defined by our work, but are encountered, freshly, frankly by those we meet.

Separated from our context, our credentials, we grow increasingly aware of who we are at the core of our being, and of what gifts are ours to give. We learn to receive others—without a home, our hospitality must be the opening of our hearts. We receive this hospitality ourselves and realize what it is to be displaced, and to be given place in the welcoming heart or home of another person. These are gifts of the Sabbath as well—the sense of coming home to, being real in, and becoming whole in a place made in time by the Lover of our souls. I hope that you will recognize the miracle of *sabbatical* in all your travels, and that the journey will become one of your Sabbath practices.

Accustomed to speeding past, losing touch with self and others, we are learning to slow down, to be still and present, to see and touch and possess the treasures on the path of process. Sabbath rest—the mind of Shalom—has this to teach our souls, and more. Through stillness we are developing an appreciation for non-doing. "Doing nothing can be a more creative act and a greater achievement than doing anything at all—and it can require far more strength, selflessness, and courage. The refusal to exercise one's own initiative too quickly can also provide others with time and space to realize their own possibilities for growth."[10]

To wait upon others, to be willing to give them place within our selves, to be affected by them, is a form of vulnerability. We literally *suffer* another person to *be*. We are "[m]ost like God not in our transformation of the world, but in our capacity to drink to the lees

10. Harned, *Patience*.

the cup of suffering it offers, not in expressing our own initiatives, but in waiting upon the initiatives of others."[11] This forbearance is not easy in the best of times, but when it seems forced upon us by circumstances or by other people, it can seem impossible to achieve.

Waiting in bumper-to-bumper traffic, in long lines, for the contributions of co-workers, for a spouse to grow, for the results of medical tests, or for any of dozens of other circumstances, we can choose proactive patience or reactive impatience—contentment or discontent. "Discontent is far from a minor sin . . . within it there is something truly satanic. Like Satan himself, the phenomena of discontent are legion: envy and anger, boredom and sloth, sadness and despair, turbulence of spirit and resentment, greed and many more, all of which are expressed in the sin of murmuring, the rejection of the quiet of the contented heart. [M]urmuring expresses continuing engagement with the world instead of disengagement from it for Christ's sake."[12]

Sabbath rest—restoration of a truly human leisure and the attitudes, perspectives and graces springing from it—is the antidote to all these "phenomena of discontent." To dwell with, to abide with others we hope to imitate Christ's patience—to be so immersed in the living waters of Sabbath that, like sopping sponges, when pressed we simply give forth the peace He has given us. The passivity that suffers the *being* of others—realities that threaten to undermine our contentment—is not the weak inactivity of a lazy, immature, or spineless soul, but the gift of self, the "agency that only grace can sustain."[13] Our waiting, our yielding, our silent suffering "are among the most significant and creative acts that we can ever undertake because of the ways they can exercise transformative power in the lives of others."[14]

The third aspect of this capacity for waiting, this patience with process, is the sense in which Scripture teaches us to wait upon the Lord. This is not the finger-drumming patience with His slowness

11. Ibid.
12. Ibid.
13. Ibid.
14. Ibid.

that we might expect. Instead, this is a waiting synonymous with hope, charged with the confident expectation that He will attend to our cry, meet us, teach us, lead us, light the way, and bring good for us out of every circumstance of life. If acedia is a form of despair, what better antidote for its poison than the hope that is the essence of this waiting? Sabbath teaches us to bear the "crisis" of slowness without impatience or despair by reminding us that God has seen fit to be "inefficient" and "impractical"—even wasteful—with time.

He has deemed it good to mediate His graces to us through the clumsiness of matter, of persons, and of human institutions. As we learn patience with ourselves and others; as we receive the sacraments; as we are molded by the Church and by Sabbath-keeping into vessels of grace, temples of the Spirit; as we learn that the feast is so much more than mere food, we become so glad for this "inefficient" and vastly slowed down "distribution system." As supernatural grace flows carefully to us through these natural "materials" of human being, perhaps it helps us to bear the "weight of glory"—like the fiber in fruit that mitigates the rush of its sugar to our bloodstream.

12 – Formed by Encounter

Make yourself a capacity, and I will make myself a torrent.
Jesus' words to Blessed Angela of Foligno

As you have studied the Sabbath with me, you have been in an encounter with both an Idea and a person; with Reality. You have sought to increase your ability to receive it by responding in intentional ways to its meaning. Each restatement of its message, each new perspective on Sabbath, provided fresh encounter with it—the growing base of familiarity increasing your capacity to grasp and retain more of the Idea. The greater your engagement with it, the more fully formed the Reality of Sabbath has become in you, the more capable you are of communicating it to others. This cycle, this process of the life-to-life transfer of what is real has everything to do with being human.

It is the movement by which a soul is formed, a person is educated, Christ is embodied, an experience becomes a poem. Fr. Luigi Giussani, in *The Risk of Education*, defines education as "the introduction to the totality of reality."[1] "Without this introduction to the totality, there is no affirmation of reality."[2] Without this affirmation, this "yes" to reality, there is no personhood, no identity. Fr. Giussani tells us that the "I" develops in response to encounter with reality. Sabbath facilitates this formation by being a context for encounter with the Person of Christ in the Eucharist, with nature, beauty, real people. To the extent it has helped you make space within your life, within your being, for such encounters, it has already begun making you more fully human, more abundantly alive.

The quiet of the rest is essential to musical composition, and the quiet of the caesura to the crafting of a poem. The composition of a

---

1. Fr. Luigi Giussani, *The Risk of Education* (New York, NY: Crossroad, 2001).
2. Ibid.

painting also makes use of the balance between positive and negative space—the image, around which surrounding space is shaped, and the emptiness which seems to beckon the form into being. So, the contemplative and active aspects of life balance one another. So, too, quietude can be seen both as an emptiness and as a fullness. We are most "composed," most centered, most poised when we most experience this balance—in a moment, and in life, as a whole. The life of activity, of ordinary days, is necessarily more full of "stuff," of material, of encounters, of demands and of movement. One single Sunday, lived without the fullness of Shabbat Shalom, is unable to balance the weight of the week. Welcomed and celebrated as Sabbath, however, Sunday (and the growing infusion of Shalom into the grind of daily days) overflows with grace sufficient to maintain our equanimity and peace throughout the week.

"Emptiness" is an interior quality of the spacious soul. To be emptied of vain imaginations, demands, attachments, and to be open—hospitable, teachable—is to possess oneself in quietness and trust. "Emptiness" speaks of what is absent, of interior simplicity, of single-mindedness. "[T]hose who complain the loudest of the emptiness of their lives are usually people whose lives are overcrowded, filled with trivial details, plans, desires, ambitions, unsatisfied cravings for passing pleasures, doubts, anxieties and fears; and these sometimes further overlaid with exhausting pleasures which are an attempt, and always a futile attempt, to forget how pointless such people's lives are. Those who complain in these circumstances of the emptiness of their lives are usually afraid to allow space or silence or pause in their lives."[3]

Emptiness in our environment—absence of noises, clutter, idle chatter—manifests and cultivates the interior spaciousness we hope will grow as we learn to value silence more and more. Our Sabbath practices may include Saturday attention to housekeeping, with an eye toward preparing homes and hearts to receive Queen Shabbat. The practice of avoiding media technologies has the dual effect of contributing to our freedom from being manipulated, and also of

3. Caryll Houselander, *The Reed of God* (Allen, TX: Christian Classics, Division of Resources for Christian Living, no date shown).

re-sensitizing us to the unprecedented levels of daily noise we take for granted. Families may want to imitate the midday Grand Silence of Benedictine monks, or their deeply calming daily cycle of the hours. Monastic life, in fact, inspired Holly Pierlot's book, *A Mother's Rule of Life*, in which she makes suggestions for bringing the insights of the cloister into home life.

"The cloister," says Esther de Waal in *Lost in Wonder*, "is one of the greatest of monastic gifts, and we should marvel not only at its beauty and its aesthetic delight but even more at its significance and what it can tell us about the way in which we shape the pattern of our lives."[4] The separation of space for emptiness, for no productive purpose, is an architectural image of the Sabbath rest, and can inform the home as well as the monastery. Wherever you can leave clean, uncluttered, even empty space within your home, you express that you value the self-collectedness of a quiet heart. Couple this with stillness, and then prayer—what Bl. Mother Teresa called the "fruit of silence"—occurs more effortlessly.

Notice two things about the quietude you are cultivating. First, that it is linked to the idea of the sabbatical journey through the concept of "vacation," whose root, "*vacate*," means to be still, empty. Second, that it is linked to the childlikeness of those who enter heaven by the idea of play. St. Thomas Aquinas considered play a kindred spirit to contemplation. Buddhists will see in this childlikeness the "beginner's mind" that is quietly focused on the task at hand and responsive to the "now" moment. Think of a child at play—wholeheartedly absorbed, unconscious of time passing, alert without anxiety or stress—to imagine this sort of playful, centered, quiet approach to the demands of the day.

In homes full of children it may be especially difficult to achieve exterior, environmental quiet, and thus more important to develop interior quietude. You will think of creative ways—on Sundays, and in Sabbath moments through the week—to quiet the place where you dwell. I say "dwell" here, because it implies an at-home-ness—a leisurely sense of spending time at home just *being*—in contrast to home as a way-station for distracted, disconnected family members

---

4. Esther de Waal, *Lost in Wonder* (Collegeville, MN: Liturgical Press, 2003).

stopping off en route to a scattering of separate *doings* elsewhere. The conscious, loving intention that creates a home of a house can also quieten it.

Teaching children not to interrupt, to walk and close doors calmly, to answer a bell or a gentle summons, to use "inside" voices, to make eye contact before speaking—all are examples of quieting practices. In my home, the "grand silence" is a daily two-hour "nap," which may be used for reading, sleeping, or other individual, still, quiet activity. In Montessori environments, children are taught to walk and move chairs with quiet deliberation, and to respect the work of others by not disrupting it with physical or aural intrusion. Non-verbal signs can reduce the need for constant practical chatter; no-media rules subdue mechanical noises during certain times, at least. All such changes, adopted initially as Sabbath practices, re-tune our ears and re-sensitize us to the impact noise elsewhere has on our ability to be inwardly hushed and open.

Heart openness is affected negatively by the noisiness of life. When we recoil against the assault of noise on our inner ear— defend ourselves from what amounts to an act of violence upon the soul—we close, to some extent, the doors of our heart. The open, quiet, centered soul is one that can maintain hospitality, transparency, vulnerability in the face of temptations to self-protectiveness. The still, silent point within us—the vessel of Shabbat Shalom—is the seed of our soul's formation. As it expands, we become place— safe harbor, shelter, womb—for Christ and for the people we encounter. "So we can see that creating space is far from easy in our occupied and preoccupied society. And still, if we expect any salvation, redemption, healing and new life, the first thing we need is an open, receptive place where something can happen to us. Hospitality, therefore, is such an important attitude."[5] If your home is not yet a sanctuary, you may need to find quietness in the sanctuary of Our Lord, in nature, or in the heart of Mary, where we are always welcome and given place to meet with Christ.

'Not only are others received into our quieted hearts, but also we

5. Henri Nouwen, *Reaching Out* (Garden City, NY: Doubleday & Company, 1975).

discover there our own selves. Finding within not a void, but a place given boundary and shape by our own being, we can explore to discover who we are. "It is not a formless emptiness, a void without meaning; on the contrary, it has a shape, a form given to it by the purpose for which it is intended,"[6] says Caryll Houselander in *The Reed of God*. Our unique emptiness may be "like the hollow in the reed" whose destiny is to sing God's song; "like the hollow in the cup, shaped to receive water or wine"; "like that of the bird's nest," shaped to receive fledgling life. The task of self-emptying is to sift and sort out "everything that is not essential and that fills up space and silence in us . . . [to discover] what sort of shape this emptiness in us, is. From this we shall learn what sort of purpose God has for us. In what way are we to fulfill the work of giving Christ life in us?"[7]

Whatever we are—male, female, old, young, strong, weak, verbal, mathematical, artistic, musical, mechanically apt, mild, or passionate—"gives form to the emptiness in us" and can show us "the way Christ wills to show Himself" in our life. The Holy Spirit is given to quicken the "stuff we are made of" to life—to burn the self we place at His disposal as a log on the fire of love—so that His love becomes light within us. Thus, breath—always a metaphor for *pneuma*, spirit—is the bridge from quiet emptiness to quiet fullness.

The value of deep, slow breathing for the relaxation and centering of both mind and body is well-documented. If we would restore, by Sabbath practice, the disintegration of our embodied souls, then the conscious practice of filling-self-with-breath (literally, a fuel for life-giving combustion and healing energy all the way through to the cellular level of our being) and conscious awareness of self-emptying—exhalation of toxins, stress, control—is a good place to begin. In each moment of the process we become more conscious that we receive ourselves, receive life, newly in each moment from the hand of God. We gradually release the illusion that we are self-sustaining, that we must "try hard" or "work hard" to exist, or to earn our being. "The movement from illusion to

6. Houselander, *The Reed of God*.
7. All in this paragraph: Houselander, *The Reed of God*.

prayer under girds and makes possible the movements to solitude and hospitality and leads us to the core of the spiritual life."[8]

Prayer moves us deeper into relationship with God—relatedness, likeness, mutuality. Formal prayer gives a structure that provides a point of entry into the practice of prayer and into the ongoing prayers of the whole Church. *Lectio divina*, for instance, is the slow, prayerful reading (of Scripture, poetry, short passages of spiritual classics) that leads "into reflection, into contemplation, into stillness until finally it explodes, and bursts into a flame of love."[9] In the *horarium*, or Office of Christian Prayer, we step into the majestic, orbital structure of the constant prayer of the Church.

Since the earliest days of the Apostles, prayer vigil has been kept round the clock, taking the form of the Office, in which Psalms, Old Testament, New Testament, writings of the saints and the canticles of Zechariah and Mary link us to the Church universal—transcending time and space. Chant is a "praying twice"[10] in which we submit to the listening required for genuine responsiveness to time, and to others. "From the monastic perspective, time is a series of opportunities, of encounters. We live in the now by attuning ourselves to the calls of each moment, listening and responding to what each hour, each situation brings. . . . Calling and responding belong to the very essence of [chant]. . . . What matters is not the singer but the song, the self-transcending responsiveness that chant demands."[11]

Self, meeting Spirit, at the center—a wick burning but not consumed as person encounters Person, and love encounters Love; Spirit burning like pure and unexhausted oxygen within the inner chamber. Only to the extent that we are *place* can this holy combustion occur (as flame cannot burn in a vacuum, in a no-where-ness). All our practices of slowness, stillness, playfulness, awareness, orderliness, and quietness contribute to the shaping of this interior chamber. All the disciplines of formal prayer and Sacrament—com-

---

8. Nouwen, *Reaching Out*.

9. de Waal, *Lost in Wonder*.

10. St. Augustine: "He who sings well prays twice."

11. David Steindl-Rast, Sharon Lebell, *Music of Silence 2 Ed.: A Sacred Journey Through the Hours of the Day* (Berkeley, CA: Ulysses Press, 2001).

munion, rosary, Divine Office, confession, Divine Mercy, fasting, chanted psalms, etc.—help us to keep it swept clean and to discover its contours. None more so than our Sabbath practices and the Sabbath Sacrament of the Eucharist.

I have called your attention to the process by which the idea of Sabbath, the Life of Christ, grows within you, taking form inwardly that moves you to outward expression and representation of the Idea. I have emphasized the interior emptiness that is an essential aspect of this process because in our culture the focus tends to be on "getting full of" things rather than on "preparing to receive" things. Nowhere is this more clear than in our approach to education. We tend to think of lists of facts or subjects as things to be poured into the minds of students as they proceed from stop to stop along the conveyor belt of education. In contrast, I hope you will notice the slow process by which you have been coming to fully grasp the Sabbath. You will be a much better teacher (of any subject) once you are conscious of the learner's need for expansion in his capacity to receive, and the restful attentiveness that makes possible a more fully integrated *knowing*.

Most of us are instrumental in the education of others in some sense—raising children, telling stories of our formative experiences, arguing to defend the Faith, teaching a friend how to bake bread, sharing tips for gardening or herbal remedies, counseling women on the way into abortion clinics. These informal teaching relationships you take for granted are really vital encounters—experiences of the person-to-person transfer of ideas—living encounter with Reality. They will seem more, or less, vital according to the importance you place on the idea you want to communicate, but all are examples of the quintessentially human work of giving to another person what is real and valued in yourself. These are instances of self-donation, of the "gift of self" that has power to help a recipient receive truth, goodness and beauty through your hands. Thus, there are no unimportant gifts of self, no meaningless encounters with Reality, no educational exchanges that don't matter vitally. Each one has the potential to be quickened into life by the Spirit of Truth.

If we take seriously the need of persons to be formed in wonder, in quietude, at a speed that is humane, in a place that is safe harbor for vulnerable souls, and in ways that promote the expansion, rather than the contraction, of the soul's capacities to know, love, serve, and create, these moments will be seen to have eternal significance. Evangelization is a particular kind of education—possibly the highest form, because by it we hope to bring another to encounter with the living Person of Christ, rather than with facts or ideas or truths about Him. We'll see next why the call to bring, not just news, but a person, reveals the highest dimension of our humanity: the capacity to create beauty.

13 – Something Beautiful for God

The better I get to know anything at all,
the more universal becomes its significance.
Cornelius Verhoeven, "The Philosophy of Wonder"

You have come so far, followed so many threads with me! From knowing by trusting, to knowing by practice, to knowing by intellect, to knowing by *person*; from laying a foundation to building the structure of the Idea, to securing your grasp of it by deeper understanding, to filling it with the pleasant riches of expanded knowledge—you have journeyed and, hopefully, been enriched along the way. Along with the expansion in your concept of Sabbath, has come enrichment of the idea of the human person. Given the freedoms and dignity that make a person *essentially* human (the image of God in him conferring his very essence), we have moved from a sense in which Sabbath rest makes a person *generally* more human, to one in which it makes him *effectively* more human. Let me explain.

Any human being, if he would rest from busyness, be more quiet, slow down, consciously live in interdependent community, think of his life as a work of art, cultivate the ability to be at leisure with himself, engage in creative re-presentation of whatever delights him, and have the courage to step out from his crippling self-defenses would truly be more human, more fully alive—all this without being ordered self-consciously toward the meaning of his existence, the purposes for which he was created. But this same, generally-fulfilled, person, given a sense of God's intention for him—to make him a knower of truth, a lover of goodness, and a creator of beauty—has a more fully formed humanity; a *being* with greater dimension, greater capacity to receive reality.

In this sense, he is now moving toward becoming more effectively human—more capable of knowing, loving and serving God, which are the attributes of the most fully human, fully alive, person. These effects, before they impact others, are first produced in him—Christ is formed in his being. The effects he becomes capable of producing in the world must first be effected within him by God's initiative and the response of his free will.

The full scope of the human person goes far beyond what we can possibly conceive, but a third dimension is within our grasp to contemplate. I call it being *specifically* human, because Pope St. John Paul II stressed the "radical specificity" of the human person. Just as Christ condescended to the utmost specificity—one human being within one specific woman at a particular point in history and in geography—and through that radically small entryway into space and time ushered in His kingdom, our own particular beings become capacities for His overflowing grace in the world. We have seen how learning to wait helps us to better accept that God has chosen to mediate His graces through human beings. We have seen how our particularity is quickened into life as our soul is educated to the Source and fullness of its being. To enter into this reality is to become more specifically human.

Thus, the fullness of what it means to be human is to be most truly *you*. We often ask what work God wants us to do, and here is the answer. He wants you to *be*. He has so designed the human person as to be His own response to the specifics of that person's actual life, times, constraints, wounds, desires, needs. Each of these represents a kind of "problem," for which you are the "solution." What you encounter meets Him—touching the hem of His garment at that radically specific moment—and His grace flows out in response through you.

Your response-ability in each present moment is a function of the wholeness of your own being and the fullness of Christ's being within you. This wholeness has to do with the integrity—purity, integration, health, connectedness, vitality—of all the elements of your being, which Sabbath exists to cultivate. You are the point of integration of all the disparate elements that meet in you—the neighborhood you live in, your genetic inheritance, the language you speak, your skills and interests, the scars you bear, your passions and weaknesses, the books you have read, etc. . . . Only *you* can make a creative response to and through the specifics of *your* encounter with reality.

To create—to re-present what is vital and well-formed within you, what you have let affect you—is to resolve the tension of the paradoxes that are met in you. Creativity *is* the resolution of paradox, and it is the most fully human calling. The poet, the artist, the composer, the home maker all create—of elements juxtaposed in some degree of tension, paradox, seeming incompatibility—a new thing: a harmonious and beautiful whole. Bl. Mother Teresa laid down her very life to "resolve the tension" between man made in the image of God and man dehumanized by neglect and poverty; she created a "new thing," a way of love, a bridge between what *is* and what should be. Human creativity corresponds to the beauty of truth, of the created world, of virtue because it involves your capacity to co-operate, to respond with God in responding to reality. So we turn at last, back to the beginning of our study of Sabbath—to the beauty of *being*, and its power to bear the Person of Christ, to regenerate the human person, and thus to bear Christ to the world.

There is a sense in which evangelization and beauty are two sides of the same coin. On the one hand, we proclaim the Good News, calling people to step inside the Church to know Him personally. ("The kingdom of God . . . is before all else a person with the face and name of Jesus of Nazareth, the image of God.")[1] On the other, immersed in the living water, we place it all around outside the Church in small containers to sustain people wherever they are. We, in whom Christ dwells, welcome the world into His heart through the hospitality of our souls, into His Church through our own homes. Through us, He says, like Dickens' Ghost of Christmas Present, "Come in, man, and know me better!"

In His rest we are awakened to wonder and restored in our capacity to translate what we perceive into words, images, buildings, poems, lives of beauty, that attract a world though its senses are dulled. This is the condescension of love—not a snobbery, aloof and proud of its superiority, but a cascade of the torrent of Christ's love downward, downward as far as necessary to reach man wherever he

1. Pope St. John Paul II, *Redemptoris Mundi*, Paragraph 18.

may be found. "The characteristic of a man who feels himself freed, saved, and therefore new, is that he gets involved in history, creating something in gladness and joy."[2]

"It is as though beautiful things have been placed here and there throughout the world to serve as small wake-up calls to perception, spurring lapsed alertness back to its most acute level."[3] A beautiful thing *is* a proclamation of the gospel message. Elaine Scarry's *On Beauty and Being Just* demonstrates the capacity of beauty to restore in some measure the beholder's, the receiver's, capacity for all beauty and thus for Christ who is, beyond all things, beautiful. Its very presence (literally, *prae sens*—standing before the senses) exerts a pressure toward justice, symmetry (both, forms of rest-full-ness) in the world around it. "Beauty is a call" from eternity, a transforming nudge that causes a "radical decentering" and leaves us "standing in a different relation to the world than we were a moment before. . . . It is not that we cease to stand at the center of the world, for we never stood there. It is that we cease to stand even at the center of our own world. We willingly cede our ground to the thing that stands before us."[4] Sabbath-keeping prepares us to receive beauty by helping us "cede our ground."

This creative destabilization gives us an important link between beauty and evangelization. Let's back up for a moment to recall the image of persons needing place within our hearts to "become," to "sound." The less whole we are, the more we will withhold our voice from the world; the less soul, the less sound; the more likely we are to either put up such walls of self-protection that the sound cannot be heard, or to let the boundaries of our own vessel crumble to the point we become mere echoes of other people. In between these extremes, most of us sound but weakly, and look to others for rein-forcement of our own voice, reassurance of our own presence in the world. We need to be pulled out, drawn out, of our self defenses to

2. Fr. Luigi Giussani, *From Utopia to the Presence* (A talk by Fr. Giussani to students in Riccione, Italy, October, 1976).

3. Elaine Scarry, *On Beauty and Being Just* (Princeton, NJ: Princeton University Press, 2001).

4. Ibid.

real encounter with everything, everyone in our path. "I need the whole world. The whole world has to be integrated in me; I need to get close to everything, to nourish myself from everything, so that in me everything can become Christian."[5]

It is natural to gravitate toward those who think like, look like, sound like us. There is positive value in affiliation. The danger is that, to the extent of our disintegration, we are off-key and thus multiplying disharmony, dissonance with the song of Sabbath. What is true, what is beautiful will now be less and less in tune with our own soul and we are likely to shut it out more and more. The person is a complex symphony of beauties and formation (or deformation) of the soul in one aspect expands (or contracts) the soul in all. "To him who has, more will be given; from him who has not, everything will be taken away."[6]

Until we can perceive this spiral of contraction and grasp the reality that many of the displaced, restless souls around us are without much capacity to receive truth, we will not realize the crying need of the world for us to make truth ever and again condensed and new—to re-present it and to place it where people might stumble over it, so that it might catch them off guard. This destabilizing moment can get the downward spiral moving in the opposite, soul-expanding direction. Now it is clear how beauty and evangelization meet within the Sabbath, in the person of the Sabbath-keeper.

What must the world be given to win it to the Lord? Beauty—in small portions, placed in every corner of the world, speaking the languages of the poor, the atheist, the rich man with an empty soul, the child, the punk, the prisoner, the orphan. These "portions" must come in a variety of shapes and sizes, but be internally consistent with the Truth, have inherent value. They will be flawed, insufficient, incomplete—good things, done badly—yet still be shards of the shattered vessel of creation. They will be ephemeral—material, lasting only briefly and quickly forgotten, decaying into the soil of

5. Fr. Divo Barsotti, quoted by Giancarlo Cesana in "The Response to a Human Need," *Traces*, Vol 8, #7, 2006.

6. Mark 4:25, "For whoever has, to him more will be given; but whoever does not have, even what he has will be taken away from him."(RSV)

things temporal. And yet the Idea, the eternal Sabbath moment, which they have carried into the world remains and has its effect.

Wait, are we talking about a person or a painting; bits of manna or Living Bread; a poem or a life? All of these! "You are God's *poema* (His *poem*, carefully crafted, every part chosen for its own sake and also for the layers of meaning it can carry for Him) created in Christ Jesus unto good works which He has prepared in advance for you to do."[7] Your life is yours to craft, and can become "something beautiful for God."[8] "Not all are called to be artists in the specific sense of the term. Yet, as Genesis has it, all men and women are entrusted with the task of crafting their own life: in a certain sense, they are to make of it a work of art, a masterpiece."[9]

Your holiness, wholeness, humanity, integrity is the most beautiful thing that has ever infiltrated the world and the only thing capable of changing it positively. Think of the array of vastly different people who all found in Bl. Mother Teresa a beauty that swept them off their feet, out of their comfort zones, and into her small-town "symphony." Love for her, unity with her is their practice, their training ground for and small taste of the experience of participating in the universal Song.

Cardinal Marc Ouellet, discussing the phenomena of the many vital new ecclesial movements, suggests that the way of beauty is the way of restored humanity:

> Is aesthetics a truly fruitful way for the Church today? . . . I could be so bold as to say, as a hypothesis, or a bet, that the way of beauty seems to be that of the ecclesial movements and the new communities. At the beginning of the new millennium, are we (perhaps) called to start off again from the beauty of Christ? The way of beauty meets the deepest aspirations of the human heart. Today it is urgent to explore this way of beauty, since the point of

---

7. Eph. 2:10, "For we are God's *workmanship* (in Greek, *poema*), created in Christ Jesus for good works, which God prepared beforehand, that we should walk in them." (RSV)

8. Bl. Mother Teresa: "To show great love for God and our neighbor we need not do great things. It is how much love we put in the doing that makes our offering something beautiful for God."

9. Pope St. John Paul II, *Letter to Artists*, April 4, 1999.

view of truth and goodness are less effective in reaching the men of today, all steeped in skepticism and relativism. Christians have the task of restoring this harmony between truth, goodness and freedom, starting off from the living encounter with Christ who reawakens man's heart and gives a meaning to his life by opening him to reality as a whole.... One of the tasks of the ecclesial movements and the new communities in the present moment of the world and of the Church is that of educating people in humanity, towards a fullness of humanity.[10]

The world needs for us to take the risk of creating beauty, of being so fully and so specifically who we really are that Christ flows out from us in new forms. "[B]eing Christian is being more. It is living more. [T]he importance of beauty means facing up to and engaging in a personal comparison with desire, inasmuch as beauty arouses desire, which is the most 'dangerous' aspect of the human experience, in that it is the least controllable."[11] The whole-mindedness with which you trust God to work even through your desires frees you, centers and stabilizes you, calls forth from within you what only you can give. Like a tree taking up inorganic materials from the soil and transforming them into its own, live, life-giving being, the human person takes up the specifics of his life and transforms them into living carriers of his being. Truly, we shall be like trees, planted by streams of living water![12]

If we would be beauty-makers—living transformers of Truth into transferable forms—we must be beauty-seekers. The initiative has been taken by God. He has lit the spark of spirit within us that Sabbath will keep alive and nurture. His beauty calls to us from the moment of conception to *be*, to seek Him where He may be found, to turn and turn again toward Him as the growing flower turns always toward the sun. Unless you can believe, as Bl. Mother Teresa

---

10. Cardinal Marc Ouellet, "The Beauty of Being Christians," *Traces*, Vol. 8, #7, 2006.

11. Giancarlo Cesana, "The Response to a Human Need," *Traces*, Vol. 8, #7, 2006.

12. Psalm 1, "Blessed is the man who walks not in the counsel of the wicked, ... but his delight is in the law of the Lord.... He is like a tree planted by streams of water, ... in all that he does, he prospers." (RSV)

did, that there is infinite beauty in a human person, you are not fully ready to evangelize. Unless you can make place within your heart for him, he may have no place in his for you.

Being *right* does not make you righteous, and knowing the truth merely intellectually is not at all the same as *bearing* it—knowing it as a person, as a Person. To "bear" is to suffer under the weight of, to give place to (as Mary weighed the angel's message, or as the word of God needs to "dwell in you richly")[13] and to be affected by the burden. A person is a precious vessel and we do him violence, injustice, if we try to take a shortcut to his soul—the casual transfer of the facts of the gospel delivered to the intellect in which so many people already hide their fractured souls, instead of the life-to-life transfusion of our own heart's blood by which they might encounter the Person of Our Lord and be made whole. Thank God there are so many of us—feeble as we tend to be—and that He "makes His strength perfect in our weakness."[14]

As you seek for beauty, you may be surprised to find great, deep pools of beauty in the works and souls of unbelievers—people ahead of you, in some sense on the path of truth, though they do not know the Person of Truth. This brings us to the Scriptural paradox that is so puzzling. "He who is not with me is against me," (Luke 11:21) and "He who is not against me is with me" (Luke 9:50). The two statements of Jesus, though they seem contradictory, are logically equivalent,[15] and thus just two ways of saying the same true thing. But our minds have difficulty accepting seeming contradiction, paradox, truth expressed as both-and. We tend to find comfort in the smallness of one extreme or the other.

In this context, we tend either to take the first statement as an

13. Col. 3:16, "Let the word of Christ dwell in you richly, as you teach and admonish one another in all wisdom, and as you sing psalms and hymns and spiritual songs with thankfulness in your hearts to God." (RSV)

14. 2 Cor. 12:9, "'[M]y power is made perfect in weakness.' I will all the more gladly boast of my weaknesses, that the power of Christ may rest upon me." (RSV)

15. Are these two statements logically equivalent? 1) "He who is not with me is against me" and 2) "He who is not against me is with me." If we let a = "not with me" and b = "against me" then statement 1 reads "if *a* then *b*" and statement 2, "if not *b* then not *a*," is its contrapositive, or logical equivalent (not not with = with).

excuse to disrespect everyone who is not "on our side" as though they were all totally against us (then, by continuing digression, not worth the time of day) or to take the second statement as cheap comfort that, no matter what our essential differences, we are all on the same side with anyone who doesn't confront us with those differences (then, by continuing digression, there is no reason whatever to practice loving condescension because all value is now flattened by a false sense of the relativity of truth.) The whole truth is that there are many people who are very, very wrong about a great many things we are right about and yet bear the image of God and are the objects of His longing and love; and also there are a great many who are very much in the path of truth and right about a great many things and yet who could stand to take lessons from people they are looking down at in a snobbishness born of insecurity.

We are a mixed bag. The soul at rest is not only able to resolve paradox creatively—responding to reality in loving affirmation—but is also more able to hold greater paradoxes in tension within himself—to see through error to the kernel of truth, to see Christ in the least spark of humanity, to trust God to "make a way where there is no way."[16] Let's find beauty wherever we can and affirm it, let it affect us, reproduce it in our lives, and let Christ be lifted up to draw all men to Himself. May your hearts be abundantly blessed as you find in Sabbath rest the Shalom of Our Lord.

We have only today. Let us begin.
Blessed Mother Teresa

---

16. Isaiah 43:19, "Behold, I am doing a new thing; now it springs forth, do you not perceive it? I will make a way in the wilderness and rivers in the desert." (RSV)

Epilogue – A Fugue on Poetry

I have set so many "themes a-playing" that perhaps your head is spinning! In the fugue which follows (my own term, not technically a poetic form) I have constrained myself to two: "man alive" and "man as place," which I then resolve into one: "man as poem." In a sense, everything in Souls at Rest *is summarized here. Only within the context of Sabbath can the paradox of man birthing at once himself, and others, be fully resolved.*

The first page of G.K. Chesterton's *Manalive* is breathtaking. Though prosaic, this is some of the finest poetry it has ever been my joy to read. One sentence must suffice: "A wind sprang high in the west like a wave of unreasonable happiness and tore eastward across England, trailing with it the frosty scent of forests and the cold intoxication of the sea." To one who knows the animating secret of this book, the words carry the thrill of bracing expectancy, though to the uninitiated they may be vaguely unsettling—like the wind-whisked central character whose sanity seems insane.

There is a day whose sanity seems insane except to the initiate. A day when time and eternity are one; when God and man are one; when I am whole, healed, wholly holy, holy. God created it and called it Sabbath. He placed His finest, fullest most refreshing rest within it to prepare a people to receive Him, to be conformed to its contours and thus to His own. He called her His bride. We know her as the Sunday of Lord Sabbaoth. The measure of our comfort and delight in her sky-opening, tree-cleaning, skirt-whipping, door-slamming weekly entrance measures us.

The wind that brings Chesterton's Innocent Smith into focus and the wind that ushers man into the Day are both winds of revolution—full of explosion, rending, disruption and invisible energy. Both refresh a man "like a flagon" and "astonish him like a blow."

Both are the stuff by which tragic dwarves become lively imps and hammocks fly us to heaven. Borne in by such a blazing breeze a person is made a deeper mystery—utterly unfathomable yet strangely simple. Onlookers may scorn him, in fact, as a simpleton, but by virtue of the Sabbath-keeper all things are made new.

To one who has experienced the oak, majestic in maturity and glorious in the fullness of its growth, the acorns lying round it are so obviously the natural scheme of its fecundity as to come as no surprise—in fact to suffer from banality itself. Yet to the child, the notion that the tiny acorn in his palm somehow contains the other Thing—the leaf and branch, nobility and essence of the oak; that his hand may contain a Being which so overtops and overshadows his own being as to make him quite unsettlingly small is a wondrous thought, indeed.

To a one-dimensional being, all other beings of whatever number of dimensions would be perceivable only as points—disconnected, unrelated, speeding around him with a frightening arbitrariness. In such a universe—a "flatland"—no continuity, consistency, or sameness could be perceived between one aspect of a thing and another. The acornness of an oak, or the oakness of an acorn, for example, would be lost. In our world the human person is being flattened into a sort of two-dimensionality-from-three and, thus reduced in capacity to perceive a sphere except as a passing line, has the spaciousness of his soul compromised.

The capacity of a soul to receive being—an idea, a thing, a person, an event—into itself in fullness is formed by wonder. To receive wholly one must first be whole. This wholeness, this interior spaciousness, this integrity is cultivated by, is actually created by awe—the desire to know whatever one encounters and the impetus to know it in its entire dimensionality. Wonder requires slowness, stillness, stopping, silence, space, safety.

Only in its embrace can the human soul exist in its fullness and thus apprehend, possess, and love all other Things. Speed disconnects, but Sabbath moments remake, reunify.

Wonder is a yearning to know what cannot yet be fully grasped—an unsettled position between encounter and complete apprehension, possession. It is short-circuited by pragmatism—putting the Thing to use flattens its inherent meaning, dulls the soul to mystery. Sabbath separation of one day for encounter between God and man and for cessation of practicality restores man to his most full humanity, to his capacity for eternity. A poem is likewise such a pause. Above all things, useless, it calls to him to see the connectedness of things—things in the nobility of true relation and relation to Truth.

Poetry connects, resolves paradox. Through metaphor, symbol, allusion and juxtaposition, the poet layers meaning upon meaning. The veil of poetry frustrates facile apprehension—by its very structure at once beckoning and denying entrance. It delivers its fullness only to patient souls willing to experience wonder—the discomfort of not knowing what belief, what faith promises can be known. Speed disconnects—destroys relationship, atomizes unity, prevents entrance into the world of meaning. Souls desperately need poetic formation to become fully Real-ized, fully human. Initiation into poetry—into the slow-knowing realm of meaning at once obscured and revealed—forms souls in Faith.

The substance of things hoped for, evidence of things unseen comes to us in a Person, as a Person. In this sense, a person is a poem—a place waiting to be filled with *being* encountered whole, to be expanded by the qualities of whatever it possesses. A poetry constrained by form is as a person constrained to the realities of physical form, weakness, circumstance, place and duty. Self-denial frees the self's true creativity. Such suffering is at the heart of beauty, of wonder, of love. Beauty breaks our hearts, in its way, and such encounter cannot be glibly reproduced.

Person is the form within which Being can be represented. If we will suffer ourselves to *be*, constrained but whole—to live as Man insanely, radically Alive—what we possess can be shared. Poetry seeks to draw another into a lived experience by reproducing the very form of the Thing it has loved in a form, a structure that makes transfer possible. Just as the word is not the thing itself, the poem is not the experience, but the place created where two multi-dimensional persons meet in wonder. Sabbath is God's poem of eternity. A poem is a Sabbath moment.

Do You Need a Speaker?

CharlotteOstermann.com

Holy Leisure is the Key to Human Being!
Holy Leisure is the Key to Human Freedom!
Holy Leisure is the Key to Human Creativity!

A Few of My Talks:

Grow Up in All Things . . . . . . for RCIA, Most Pure Heart of Mary
Sabbath: As Easy as A, B, C . . . . . . for Daughters of Isabella, KCK
Beauty Becomes You . . . . . . for Blessed Sacrament Homeschoolers
Building the Bridge . . . . for KS Homeschool Conference
Hi-Resolution Beauty . . . . for Apostles of the Interior Life Retreat
The Holy Spirit Wants You! . . . . Women of St. Ignatius
The Poetic Reader . . . . for Ladies Literary Society

CPSIA information can be obtained
at www.ICGtesting.com
Printed in the USA
FFOW03n0517271116
29711FF